Endorsements

This stimulating collection of addresses from the 100th anniversary celebration of Columbia International University invites individual believers, missions team leaders, pastors, missions agency strategists, missions workers in all their increasingly infinite variety, theological educators, and all who care about the Great Commission to zoom in on practical insights and best practices in a wide range of regions and specialties within global missions, and to zoom out to overriding questions, concepts, trends and stunning emerging opportunities. It encourages healthy and crucial reflection, re-evaluation, and either re-affirmation or humble and deliberate course correction.

Each reader will emerge better able to answer the concluding challenge from Steve Richardson, "How can I most strategically align my [individual or collective] background, talents, and resources with God's redemptive plan?" Can there be a more compelling question for those who recognize that the goal of all human history is persons from all tribes, peoples, and languages worshipping the Lamb?

Pat Hatch
Refugee and Immigrant Ministry Director,
PCA Mission to North America

This book is a delightful account of the learnings and reflections of several practitioners of mission in our contemporary era. It covers a wide variety of perspectives and provides fresh insights in the reality and practice of mission today. Anyone who desires to glance through the new expressions of mission in an era where mission has multiple centers of influence all over the world must read this book.

Michel Kenmogne, PhD
Executive Director, SIL International

This collection of reflections on missions allows you to hear from missionaries who have worked in some of the most fascinating—and often troubled—parts of the world. They have also been engaged in very diverse types of missionary work, from art therapy to medical missions, to Bible translation, to teaching in public universities overseas. But they all share some connection to Columbia International University, which—as this book reveals—is a global leader in missiology. And they all reveal their passion here to see "the nations be glad" in Jesus Christ. The story-telling style of the book is attention-grabbing, yet each author blends narrative with current missiological theory. If you are interested in missions, you will learn from this book, and you will find inspiration from it.

Kenneth Nehrbass, PhD
Associate Professor of Global Studies, Rawlings School of Divinity,
Liberty University

As missions continues to shift and regularly faces new challenges, churches and missionaries alike continually seek relevant and timely resources. *Mission in Praise, Word, and Deed* is that resource for today. By reflecting upon a variety of missions related topics, the contributors in this book offer a distinct look at where missions has been and where it is headed. The rich contextual and ministerial diversity of the contributors brings the world to the reader and encourages us all that God's work is indeed extending to every region of the world through his multifaceted plans. Through all this, this book expands our perspective on missions and will inspire us all to creatively think on and do missions more effectively during our present time and the time to come.

Michael A. Ortiz, PhD
VP for Global Ministries and Associate Professor of Missiology
and Intercultural Studies, Dallas Theological Seminary
Executive Director, International Council for Evangelical Theological Education

Great legacies do not petrify through the passage of time, rather they transition with integrity. Whether in periods of peace, war, opposition, or disruption, they refuse to compromise values even as they adjust and broaden to new realities with new partners. That's what you will discover in *Mission in Praise, Word, and Deed*. With each turn of this jewel, the reader will be reminded of past values being lived out a century later in ever-expanding ministries with those now representing the nations. What a legacy for the next century or until His return.

Tom Steffen, DMiss
Professor Emeritus, Intercultural Studies, Biola University
Co-author, *The Return of Oral Hermeneutic*

Mission in Praise Word and Deed

Reflections on the Past and Future of Global Mission

Edward L. Smither & Jessica A. Udall, editors

Available at missionbooks.org

Mission in Praise, Word, and Deed: Reflections on the Past and Future of Global Mission
© 2023 by Edward L. Smither and Jessica A. Udall. All Rights Reserved.

No part of this book may be reproduced, stored in a retrieval system, or transmitted in any form or by any means—electronic, mechanical, photocopy, recording, or otherwise—without prior written permission from the publisher, except brief quotations used in connection with reviews. For permission, email permissions@wclbooks.com. For corrections, email editor@wclbooks.com.

William Carey Publishing (WCP) publishes resources to shape and advance the missiological conversation in the world. We publish a broad range of thought-provoking books and do not necessarily endorse all opinions set forth here or in works referenced within this book. WCP can't verify the accuracy of website URLs beyond the date of print publication.

Scripture quotations marked ESV are taken from the ESV® Bible (The Holy Bible, English Standard Version®), Copyright © 2001 by Crossway, a publishing ministry of Good News Publishers. Used by permission. All rights reserved.

Scripture quotations marked NIV are taken from the Holy Bible, New International Version®, NIV®. Copyright © 1973, 1978, 1984, 2011 by Biblica, Inc.™ Used by permission of Zondervan. All rights reserved worldwide. www.zondervan.com. The "NIV" and "New International Version" are trademarks registered in the United States Patent and Trademark Office by Biblica, Inc.™

Scripture quotations marked NASB are taken from the NASB® New American Bible®, Copyright © 1960, 1971, 1977, 1995, 2020 by The Lockman Foundation. Used by permission. All rights reserved. lockman.org.

Scripture quotations marked CEV are taken from the Contemporary English Version Copyright © 1991, 1992, 1995 by American Bible Society. Used by Permission.

Published by William Carey Publishing
10 W. Dry Creek Cir., Littleton, CO 80120 | www.missionbooks.org
William Carey Publishing is a ministry of Frontier Ventures
Pasadena, CA | www.frontierventures.org

Cover and Interior Designer: Mike Riester

ISBNs: 978-1-64508-513-3 (paperback)
       978-1-64508-515-7 (epub)

Printed Worldwide   27 26 25 24 23   1 2 3 4 5   IN

Library of Congress Control Number: 2023944619

Contents

Preface   viii
    Edward L. Smither

Introduction: Trends in the Past and Future of Mission   xi
    Robert J. Priest

Part One: Mission in Praise   1

Chapter 1: The Future of Mission Is Local Worship   3
    Robin P. Harris

Chapter 2: Trauma Care and the Arts in Mission   17
    Wendy Atkins

Chapter 3: Prayer and Spiritual Warfare in Global Mission   25
    David Cashin and Victor H. Cuartas

Part Two: Mission in Word—Evangelism   33

Chapter 4: Evangelism in One Verse   35
    Bill Jones

Chapter 5: Evangelism in a Secular World   45
    Raphael Anzenberger

Chapter 6: Gospel-Centered Relationships with Muslims   53
    Trevor Castor

Chapter 7: Building God's Kingdom in Public Universities   61
    Danny McCain

Part Three: Mission in Word—Discipleship and Training   69

Chapter 8: Experiencing the Adventure of Bible Translation   71
    Ted B. Wingo

Chapter 9: Informal Theological Education: 79
    The Case of Shepherds Global Classroom
    Timothy Keep

Chapter 10: Critical Shifts: Lessons in Church Planting in Europe   87
    Dietrich Schindler

Chapter 11: Coaching Church Planters in Central Europe,   95
    Russia, and Central Asia
    Rick Amos

Part Four: Mission in Deed — 103

Chapter 12: Mission as Transformation: Five Critical Elements — 105
Bekele Shanko

Chapter 13: We Cracked the Code: — 117
Lessons Learned in Business as Mission
Brent McHugh

Chapter 14: Long-Term Medical Mission in the Middle East — 125
Dae-Young Lee

Chapter 15: Best Practices in Short-Term Medical Mission — 133
Jill McElheny

Chapter 16: Best Practices for Refugee Ministry in the Middle East — 141
Jairo de Oliveira

Part Five: The People of Praise, Word, and Deed in Mission — 149

Chapter 17: Revitalizing the House Church Tradition: — 151
A Viable Path for the Churches in China
Zhiqiu Xu

Chapter 18: From South to North: — 159
Sub-Saharans in the Mission of God
William A. Brown

Chapter 19: Lessons Learned on Multicultural Teams — 167
Sean Christensen

Chapter 20: Majority World Partnerships in Mission — 177
Ken Katayama

Part Six: Final Reflections — 185

Chapter 21: A Piece in God's Global Mission Puzzle — 187
Steve Richardson

Contributors — 195

Preface

Edward L. Smither

God is a missionary God who invites his people, the church, to participate in his mission. I define mission as crossing boundaries between the people of God and the not-yet people of God. While we cross cultural and linguistic barriers to "declare [God's] glory among the nations" (Ps 96:3 NIV), the greatest barriers we cross are faith boundaries.

In the fall of 2022, Columbia International University began its centennial year by hosting a global mission consultation. One of CIU's core values remains world evangelization, and thousands of alumni have gone to serve Christ in mission around the world, so we decided to focus the conference on the past and future of global mission. Since nearly all of the plenary and workshop speakers were CIU alumni, we essentially invited them to report on how they had been participating in the mission of God and to reflect on mission moving forward. This volume is the fruit of those presentations.

Both the conference and this book on the past and future of mission are framed around three major themes—praise, Word, and deed. We are convinced that praise (doxology) is the beginning and end of mission. John Piper famously wrote, "Missions exists because worship doesn't. Worship is ultimate, not missions, because God is ultimate, not man. When this age is over, and the countless millions of the redeemed fall on their faces before the throne of God, missions will be no more."[1] We strive to make disciples of all nations because we want to put an end to *unworship* because God is worthy to be praised by all of his creation. We also know that when people encounter the living God in saving faith and begin to worship, their lives are transformed, and they flourish.

Though mission exists because worship doesn't, Chris Wright also notes that mission exists "because praise does."[2] When we meet God in worship—when we "taste and see that the Lord is good" (Ps 34:8 NIV)—we cannot keep it to ourselves, and we're compelled to share. So, Piper rightly refers to worship as the "fuel for missions."[3] The best thing that tired and discouraged missionaries can do is maintain a daily commitment to praise and worship.

---

1 Piper, *Nations Be Glad*, 1.

2 Wright, *Mission of God*, 134.

3 Piper, *Nations Be Glad*, 1.

In mission, we proclaim the good news that Christ has died, and Christ has risen. We invite the whole world to respond in faith and follow Jesus. Though I'm persuaded that mankind's greatest needs are spiritual needs (so we must proclaim Christ), in mission, we also minister to the whole person. We care about physical, emotional, and economic needs as well as spiritual needs. Jesus healed the sick and fed the hungry while also proclaiming the kingdom of God. From a foundation of praise, we join God in his mission in Word (proclaiming) and in deed (caring for human needs).

Mission, of course, is about people. Who are the people of mission today? They are Central Asian church planters, Chinese house church pastors, and believing Filipino immigrants working in the Middle East. The majority of Christians and missionaries today come from the Global South—Asia, Africa, and Latin America. As a result, many mission teams today are multi-cultural and must learn to serve well together in the work of mission. Christian mission does not flow from the "West to rest" but from "everywhere to everyone."[4]

The authors in this volume represent the diversity of the global church on mission. They include men and women from Africa, Asia, Latin America, North America, and Europe who have served or presently serve in places like Ethiopia, Indonesia, Mexico, Haiti, Russia, France, Germany, Canada, and the regions of Central Asia, North Africa, and the Middle East. While some of our authors are scholars and even professors of mission and intercultural studies, most are field practitioners—evangelists, church planters, Bible translators, medical professionals, refugee workers, and community development specialists. Based on decades of faithful service, they are reporting on what they have learned about mission. And they convey thoughts, convictions, and vision for the future of mission as well.

A final caveat: though this volume represents a variety of approaches to mission, in no way does it claim to be a comprehensive discussion of mission. The greatest challenge in putting together the conference and then this book was knowing what would inevitably be left out. Please don't look at this book as an exhaustive guide to mission, but rather the start of a conversation. Do you see something missing or incomplete? Then please add your chapter in the ongoing discussion about the past and future of global mission.

---

4 See further Escobar, *New Global Mission*.

Bibliography

Escobar, Samuel. *The New Global Mission: The Gospel from Everywhere to Everyone.* Downers Grove, IL: IVP Academic, 2003.

Piper, John. *Let the Nations Be Glad: The Supremacy of God in Missions.* Grand Rapids, MI: Baker, 1993, 2022.

Wright, Christopher J. H. *The Mission of God: Unlocking the Bible's Grand Narrative.* Downers Grove, IL: IVP Academic, 2006.

Introduction

Trends in the Past and Future of Mission

Robert J. Priest

Christianity is a religion made to travel. The God of the Bible is not a geographically parochial deity but the Creator of the universe who desires relationship with all people. Followers of Jesus are commanded to go and serve as witnesses of Jesus and his gospel to the ends of the earth. Travel is a part of Christian faithfulness.

Travel

The Apostle Paul, benefitting from Roman roads, Roman peace, and a common language, traveled ten thousand miles as a missionary, equivalent to the distance from Eugene, Oregon, to Pretoria, South Africa. In 1793, it took the British missionary William Carey five months to travel to India. When my grandfather, Robert C. McQuilkin, was born, people were enjoying Jules Verne's 1873 science fiction *fantasy* of someone traveling around the world in *only* eighty days. As founding president of Columbia Bible College (later renamed Columbia International University, CIU) with the motto "To Know Him and Make Him Known," McQuilkin helped train generations of students, including his own children, who traveled as missionaries to distant places around the world. New technologies were greatly increasing the pace and ease of travel. For the first time in 1928, five years after CIU was founded, and just before my own mother's birth, a traveler circumnavigated the globe more quickly than the moon's twenty-seven-day orbit. Today, many reading this book have traveled farther on a single week-long mission trip than Paul, the great missionary traveler, did in his entire life.

Missionary travel has often involved dangerous adventures. Paul reported that in his "frequent journeys" he experienced hunger and thirst, sleepless nights, danger from robbers, from rivers, at sea, in cities, in the wilderness, from Gentile lynch mobs and Jewish adversaries. He was shipwrecked three times and adrift a night and day on the open sea (2 Cor 11:23–28).

In the early 1950s when my own father entered Bolivia with Cal Hibbard as the first two Wycliffe/SIL members in the country, government permissions soon allowed a whole team of SIL members—backed with ham radios and airplanes—to enter and set up shop. As a then unmarried man, my father's first job was to travel on foot, by canoe, or on ox-back through swamp and jungle, seeking to make contact with remote ethnolinguistic groups with whom language work and Bible translation could begin. I grew up hearing about his adventures while on these trips.

When I was fifteen, I went on a similar trip, sent to check out a rumor about an uncontacted indigenous group. For three weeks, Dan Gabler and I hiked through trackless mountain jungles from the town of Apolo to the mouth of the Colorado Chico River on the Peruvian border. We had close encounters with jaguars, insects, and treacherous mountain rivers. At one point, hungry and out of food, we seriously thought about eating a vulture Dan had shot. At the mouth of the Colorado Chico, we took advantage of a sand and rock bar to prepare a landing strip for a Helio Courier to pick us up and drop off another team to continue the survey upriver. I flew away, covering in minutes the sixty-seven miles it had taken weeks to traverse on foot.

Of course, missionaries and their kids are not the only ones who travel. Ten years after my own trip, Yossi Ghinsberg and three companions, having heard rumors about an uncontacted tribe with treasures of gold on the Colorado Chico River, flew to the town of Apolo and began the same trek we had traveled ten years earlier.[1] They also had experiences with jaguars, insects, raging rivers, and hunger. Yossi reported, "when you reach that level of hunger, nothing is disgusting. I would have eaten anything, even human flesh."[2]

But while Dan and I, in daily radio contact with headquarters, survived together and unscathed, Yossi and his three companions were separated. One escaped the jungle on his own and organized a rescue effort. But only Yossi was rescued. The other two were never found. As I read Yossi's book about these events and watched Daniel Radcliffe play the role of Yossi in the corresponding movie *Jungle* (2017), I reflected that if they'd just checked with me, I could have told them what SIL had already discovered: that despite rumors of an uncontacted tribe on the Colorado Chico, no such group existed—with or without treasures of gold.

---

1 See further Ghinsberg, *Jungle*.
2 Quoted in Katz, "Lost in the Jungle."

Missionary narratives of a century ago were often travel narratives. For example, in several books with titles such as *Boot and Saddle in Africa*, my grandmother's brother, Dr. Thomas Lambie, recounted his missionary travel adventures crisscrossing Ethiopia and Sudan.[3] Today's missionaries no longer face the same travel challenges earlier missionaries faced.

Language Learning

Of course, Jesus's call to go was never merely a call to travel—a religious justification for adventure tourism. It was instead a call to engage people in destination sites with a message—not in a heavenly language, but earthly. And the peoples of earth did not speak one language, but thousands. Thus, obedience to Christ's go command required language learning. Even when it took missionaries months of travel to meet distant people face-to-face, missionaries quickly learned that the last eighteen inches represented the greatest distance of all—a linguistic distance that would require not days or weeks to cross but years and even decades.

My parents were part of a missionary generation that consciously focused not simply on geographic movement but on reaching every ethnolinguistic people group in their own language. My parents studied linguistics and spent over thirty years with a few hundred Sirionó. They analyzed the language, developed an alphabet, opened a school, and translated the Bible. The story of Christian missions is a story of the greatest linguistic translation movement in history[4]—carried out by thousands of missionaries in out-of-the-way places. In the process, many missionaries, including CIU graduates such as Mary Ruth Wise and Mildred Larsen, became some of the world's greatest linguists. Linguistics is part of faithfulness to Jesus's call to go.

Culture Learning

As missionaries attempted to bridge the last eighteen inches, they discovered that language was intertwined with another barrier: culture. The fact that over half the world's languages did not have a word for kissing was an artifact not just of language but of culture. More than half the world's cultures historically did not have kissing as a cultural practice, so of course, they did not have a word for something that to them did not exist. As missionaries learned, people in specific ethnolinguistic groups shared not only language but cultural practices, beliefs, rituals, values,

---

3 See also Lambie, *Doctor without a Country* and *Doctor Carries On*.
4 See further Sanneh, *Translating the Message*.

categories, assumptions, symbols, aesthetic judgments, musical systems, worldviews, and foodways. This reality had profound implications for missionaries. When Jesus told seventy-two of his Jewish disciples preaching in Jewish villages that anytime someone welcomes you into their home and serves you food, you should "eat what is set before you" (Luke 10:8 ESV)—doing so was not culturally difficult since all parties were Jewish and thus shared dietary preferences and taboos. But when the Apostle Paul, speaking about missionary witness to Gentiles, told Jewish Christians invited to a meal by non-Christian Gentile hosts to "eat whatever is set before you" (1 Cor 10:27 ESV), compliance was profoundly difficult for Jewish believers. Would-be Jewish missionaries were naturally inclined to be Judaizers, to use Paul's word (Gal 2:14), ethnocentrically abominating the cultural practices of others and trying to make the whole world Jewish. Paul called instead for missionaries who would themselves adjust culturally—becoming "all things to all people" (1 Cor 9:22 ESV).

In Paul's paradigm, missionaries have no mandate to advocate that the world adopt the missionary's language or culture. Missionaries themselves must make cultural adjustments to others. This acculturation is part of the going that Jesus demands of us. And just as there is a science of language in linguistics, so there is a science of culture in anthropology. Indeed, missionaries were among the earliest contributors to the discipline of anthropology. Each of my parents studied anthropology and published brief articles on Sirionó culture in the premier journal *American Anthropologist*. Their goal? Not to achieve academic status but to understand another culture well enough to minister effectively and respectfully to people in that culture. So central is the anthropological concept of culture to missionary preparation today that most academic programs for missionary preparation are identified as "intercultural studies."

My parents were part of what the great missiologist Ralph Winter called "the third era" of Protestant mission, based on a paradigm of mission focused not merely on geographic movement as in earlier eras of Christian mission, but on unreached ethnolinguistic people groups. When my parents first went to Bolivia, there were many such groups without an indigenous church or Bible in their language. When SIL left Bolivia in the mid-1980s, each people group had an indigenous church and Scriptures in their language. With mission understood as initial outreach to unreached groups, my parents and their colleagues understood their task in Bolivia as completed, so they redeployed to start over elsewhere. Bolivia no longer fit the paradigm of third-era mission. Today few regions on earth truly do.

Globalization

When I did my PhD in anthropology at UC Berkeley, anthropologists mostly did not consider Christianity a suitable research topic. However, as my fellow grad students returned from fieldwork around the world, virtually every one expressed surprise that a proportion of even the most remote indigenous people they'd studied were energetic Christians. Of course, Christianity was only one globalizing element that was dramatically changing the world with reference to distinct cultures.

In 1955, Kewa New Guinea villagers, on first seeing pictures of a man and woman kissing, gasped to missionary Karl Franklin, "They're, they're, they're eating each other!" In 1976, as I traveled in the rainforest with a band of Sirionó on trek, I observed Raul attempt over several days to instruct his giggling young Sirionó bride in the revolutionary new practice of kissing. She was a willing learner. Today, it would be hard to find any society on earth where people do not, at some level, know about the cultural practice of kissing. Globalization changes cultures.

In the past, anthropologists studied local communities whose members shared a language and a unique culture. They focused especially on the cultures of discrete people groups, demonstrating the symbolic coherence, functionality, and significance of each culture. They stressed that there is more than one way of being human, and that anthropology can help us interact with people of other societies in a way that truly understands their cultural, moral and symbolic order. They described how we should not simply react ethnocentrically to cultural "others." Missionaries of that era, like my parents, found anthropology enormously helpful as they worked to communicate effectively and to inspire a contextualized, indigenous church for each culture.

But under the ongoing impact of globalization, local languages have become less salient, less likely to be the exclusive means of communication for minority populations, with regional and world languages becoming more central. When my parents began work in Bolivia, most Sirionó were monolingual—able to communicate fluently only with a population of four hundred other people. Today, few Sirionó under the age of thirty even speak Sirionó. It is instead Spanish fluency that permits engagement with a globalized world. Even among larger ethnolinguistic groups, such as Kenya's Kikuyu, Kamba, Luhya, Luo, or Kalenjin, fluency in English and perhaps Swahili, rather than one's ancestral language, are most critical to success. Increasingly, regional and international trade languages are the valued mediums of communication and knowledge in a globalized and globally networked world.

In our age of rapid transportation, instant communication, widely spoken regional and world languages, mass media presence, worldwide economic integration, and state-controlled education, old cultural systems disintegrate. Selected cultural artifacts that can be sold to tourists or selected cultural symbols that can be deployed in political contexts as markers of ethnic identity sometimes remain—but traditional cultures as intact and meaningful systems lose efficacy in the context of these other economic, political, and structural forces. This new reality creates a crisis for both anthropologists and missionaries in terms of how they conceive their task.

As anthropologists continue to research peoples they've always studied, they no longer find themselves impressed with the power and resilience of each group's culture to provide people with successful and meaningful lives. Instead, they are struck by how many of these people, in the twilight of old cultures, and under new globalized political economies, are living lives of suffering. People living in poverty, pain, and under conditions of violence or oppression is now the central focus of most anthropology, according to noted anthropologist Joel Robbins, as exposited in his already classic essay "Beyond the Suffering Subject."[5] In an equally influential article, Sherry Ortner labels this turn within anthropology as a turn towards "dark anthropology." Ortner says that, inspired theoretically by Karl Marx, anthropologists increasingly stress the harsh and brutal dimensions of social experience and view the world theoretically almost entirely in terms of power, exploitation, and chronic, pervasive inequality.[6] What this means, according to Robbins, is that most anthropologists no longer focus on culture and meaning as primary to their object of study, but instead on suffering.[7]

Interestingly, in this changing world, missionaries have also revised missionary priorities. A shrinking proportion of missionaries today fit the "third era" paradigm of pioneer mission to unreached ethnolinguistic groups with the goal of a translated gospel and founding of a viable indigenous church. This decline is true both because of earlier missionary successes in reaching such groups and because globalization is creating a different sort of world with fewer boundaries tied to language and traditional culture. Under globalization, people of all nationalities and ethnicities, many of them Christian, are in motion from everywhere to everywhere.

---

5   See further Robbins, "Beyond the Suffering Subject," 448.

6   See further Ortner, "Dark Anthropology," 50.

7   See further Robbins, "Beyond the Suffering Subject" and "Where Is the Good?"

Christian Mission Today

Space precludes a full exposition of what the Christian missionary enterprise looks like today. But whatever else is involved, the following are key parts of the pattern.

Suffering

Missionaries of the past often worked in ways intended to address suffering. A century ago, my great uncle Thomas Lambie started two hospitals in Ethiopia, one of them a leprosarium; and in Palestine, he founded a tuberculosis sanitarium. My mother, a registered nurse, spent much of every day attending to the medical needs of the Sirionó—just as her sister Aimee, also a missionary nurse, did for forty years in Colombia, South America.[8] Through my parents' ministry, the Sirionó moved in three decades from illiteracy to high levels of literacy and ability to calculate finances—both of which were critical to buffering them from exploitation-induced suffering. Even today, because of bee-keeping skills they learned from my father, some Sirionó earn good income by selling honey. In the past however, it was less common to explicitly frame one's overarching missionary purpose in terms of alleviating suffering.

Dr. Ralph Winter, who named the "third era" of Protestant mission as focused on unreached peoples, suggested late in his life that we are now entering a "fourth era" of mission—a kingdom era in which we must reconceptualize Christian mission as prioritizing the fight against disease, poverty, injustice, and oppression.[9] The Bible speaks about care for the suffering of the poor and oppressed, the widow and orphan, and the stranger or immigrant in our midst, and we worship a Savior who has suffered on our behalf and who calls us into a life where faithfulness involves suffering. A core aspect of gospel witness is visible love demonstrated in practical care and concern for the "least of these," so there are certainly biblical grounds for a prioritized concern for those who suffer. Scott Moreau, in analyzing current trends for the *Mission Handbook*, has demonstrated a reorientation among even older mission agencies towards contexts characterized by suffering—and thus with ministry focused on trauma care, orphan care, child sponsorship, medical missions, peace and reconciliation, relief and development, business as mission, and justice initiatives related to such

---

8 Cartee, *Señorita Aimee*.
9 See further Winter, "Seven Men, Four Eras," 308–16.

things as sex trafficking.[10] Under the rhetoric of holistic mission, ministries to suffering people inspire a high proportion of Christian mission today.

Under globalization, the configuration of the world has changed in terms of the social location of Christians—which influences ministry patterns. We currently live in a world where a high proportion of the world's Christians reside in settings characterized by extreme poverty and suffering, while at the same time, a high proportion of the world's Christian wealth is held in other regions (such as the USA) by a sub-set of the world's Christians.[11] In large part, the goal of holistic ministry is for Christians in resource-rich parts of the world—who disproportionately own a majority of the world's Christian wealth—to partner with suffering fellow believers across economic divides to promote human flourishing and enhance the witness of local believers in their own settings. Under the current rubric of holistic mission, Western missionaries of today are most clustered not where Christians are most absent but where people live under conditions of poverty and suffering. Today, the divide between missionary sending lands and their fields of missionary attention is often a socioeconomic divide more than a religious one. Most American missionaries travel to settings where Christian presence and witness is not more absent than it is in the USA, but where the poverty and suffering are notably higher. Indeed, the very logic of holistic mission almost definitionally presupposes missionary care across such a socio-economic divide. American missionaries with a core paradigm of holistic mission are far more likely to cluster in Guatemala, for example, where poverty is high and social services are low, than in Norway where Norwegians have higher wealth, on average, than Americans, and more robust social services. This prioritization occurs even though the proportion of practicing Christians is dramatically lower in Norway than in Guatemala. Naturally, this raises important questions about core mission priorities.

Partnership

Under globalization, people of all nationalities and ethnicities, many of them Christian, are in motion from everywhere to everywhere. In nearly every ethnolinguistic group today, one finds those who are educated, bilingual (fluent in some major world language as well as their ancestral language), and often some who are Christian as well. Ministries that require fluency in such

---

10 See further Moreau, "Survey in Perspective."

11 Wuthnow, *Boundless Faith*.

minority languages, whether for outreach or Bible translation, are generally best carried out by indigenous bilingual Christians already fluent in the target language, with foreign missionaries often serving as partners, consultants, and brokers. Contemporary foreign missionaries are far less likely to acquire fluency in smaller minority languages than missionaries of the past.

In the contemporary world, Christians of all different ethnicities exist worldwide. Such Christians are themselves widely networked across regional, national, and international boundaries—each with their own mix of linguistic strengths, economic resources and constraints, and ethnic and racial identities. In such a world, those who travel and bear witness to Jesus come from all different ethnicities, nationalities, socio-economic backgrounds, religious backgrounds, and racial identities. Further, they are differentially positioned in terms of the sorts of knowledge they have (cultural, linguistic, medical, etc.) and the resources to which they have access.

Partnerships of various kinds lie at the heart of most successful Christian mission in the world today. Consider the highland Quechua of Peru. There have long been evangelical Christian churches among the Quechua, as well as popular Christian Quechua music groups employing indigenous Quechua music and instruments, with Bible translation available in various Quechua dialects. In one sense, then, it is not helpful to consider the Quechua as "unreached." But there are many individual Quechua villages scattered throughout the Andes without any church or believers present. Thus many villages can be said to be "unreached." However, it would be a poor strategy to expect to reach such villages by recruiting a swarm of North Americans to go through the lengthy process of Quechua language and culture learning to reach each such village. Consider instead the strategy of *"Misión AMEN"*—a Peruvian mission, made up of Peruvian believers, many of them already fluent in Quechua from birth, as well as in Spanish. I was able to observe a team of roughly sixty committed *AMEN* missionaries, themselves living in relative poverty, who had strategized to reach a larger town for outreach. Initially, the town mayor refused to allow them ministry access. But when the *"Misión AMEN"* arranged a partnership with forty-seven visiting medical personnel from churches in Kentucky (only a few of whom spoke Spanish, and none of whom spoke Quechua), and jointly offered a medical mission, the town welcomed all 107 missionaries with open arms—and a church was planted.

Culture

In a globalized world, according to anthropologist Joel Robbins, anthropologists have not only prioritized a focus on suffering—

understood largely as caused by economic and political forces—but they simultaneously have almost entirely dropped their earlier focus on culture and meaning.[12] Robbins asserts that anthropologists came to view politics, power, and the body as real and to throw into a "box marked unreal ... things like culture, meaning, and shared ideals."[13] Not surprisingly, under this approach, culture and meaning largely disappeared from the analysis. Missionaries have likewise struggled to make sense of human realities under globalization in terms of culture. But while specific old meanings of old cultural groups often do lose power under globalization, Robbins argues that people continue to need meaning, to create meaning, and to act in terms of meanings, values, and purposes that are cultural but reformulated in modern, globalized contexts. Suffering itself motivates meaning creation. People everywhere struggle to make sense of and respond to misfortune. Both meaning and culture remain to be understood.

Six years ago, I spent a month in Kinshasa, the third largest city in Africa—a city filled with tragedy, and where residents often explain their misfortune as caused by family members who are witches with evil preternatural powers. As part of my research, I spent four hours a day for twenty days discussing with elderly native speakers the translation of the Bible into twenty different Congolese languages, exploring especially the meaning of words in each language related to witchcraft. Each cultural group had distinct differences of belief and practice related to witchcraft. These elderly informants were often accompanied by their urban adult grandchildren who were fluent, not in their ancestral languages, but mainly in Lingala and French, the languages of business, education, and church life. These younger adults had little understanding of the distinctive cultural beliefs and practices of their own particular ancestral tribes. I lack time to explain fully, but can illustrate one shift. In the past, if you asked people to identify a life-destroying witch, in most groups, the answer would have been a poor, elderly widowed woman. Today, in Kinshasa, the answer would likely be a child—usually from a home lacking the presence of one or both biological parents, either because of parental death, marital breakups, or out-of-wedlock births. Not surprisingly, such accused children comprise the bulk of Kinshasa's tens of thousands of homeless street children.[14] Today, new cultural ideas about child witches pioneered

---

12 Robbins, "Beyond the Suffering Subject."
13 Robbins, "Where Is the Good?" 35–36.
14 See further Priest, Ngolo, and Stabell, "Child Witches in Kinshasa."

in Kinshasa, and spread through Congolese and Nigerian films, as well as through church networks, are being embraced by distant people who only a few years earlier laughed at the very idea of child witches. Young adults of Kinshasa share with each other a set of cultural assumptions about child witches as causes of contemporary misfortune but differ from their ancestors in terms of many specific cultural beliefs about witches. But they also differ *culturally* at fundamental levels from contemporary young adults in New York, Tokyo, or Seoul—most of whom would never imagine misfortune as caused by the preternatural powers of evil child witches who are relatives of the sufferer.

Cultural meanings in the modern world involve reformulations of old meanings and new mixtures (hybridities), propagated within new communication networks, and are usually discontinuous in some respects from old cultural meanings. But whether such meanings pertain to witches or to sexuality (a core area in which cultural meanings are being reformulated globally), it is possible to study them as cultural realities. Missionaries who lack tools for understanding such cultural dynamics in the modern world remain seriously handicapped in terms of effective ministry. Missiology still requires attention to cultural dynamics, but with methods and theories suitable for studying culture in the contemporary world.

Conclusion

A great deal more could be said about Christian mission in the contemporary world. One helpful way to get a sense of the range of focus in Christian mission today is simply to read the other chapters of this book which exemplify the wide array of ministries that Christian missionaries currently pursue.

Bibliography

Cartee, Marguerite McQuilkin. *Señorita Aimee*. N.p.: Latin America Mission, 2002.

Ghinsberg, Yossi. *Jungle: A Harrowing True Story of Survival in the Amazon*. New York: Skyhorse Publishing, 2009.

Katz, Isaac. "Lost in the Jungle." *Ami Magazine*. March 14, 2018. https://www.amimagazine.org/2018/03/14/lost-in-the-jungle/.

Lambie, Thomas A. *Boot and Saddle in Africa*. New York: Revell, 1943.

Lambie, Thomas A. *A Doctor Carries On*. New York: Revell, 1942.

Lambie, Thomas A. *A Doctor without a Country*. New York: Revell, 1939.

Moreau, Scott. "Putting the Survey in Perspective." In *Mission Handbook: U.S. and Canadian Protestant Ministries Overseas 2007–2009*. Edited by Linda Weber, 34–95. Wheaton, IL: Billy Graham Center, 2010.

Ortner, Sherry B. "Dark Anthropology and Its Others: Theory since the Eighties." *HAU: Journal of Ethnographic Theory* 6, no. 1 (2016): 47–73.

Priest, Anne. "Method of Naming Among the Sirionó Indians." *American Anthropologist* (Oct 1964): 1149–51.

Priest, Perry N. "Provision for the Aged among the Sirionó Indians of Bolivia." *American Anthropologist* (October 1966): 1245–47.

Priest, Robert J., Abel Ngolo, and Timothy Stabell. "Christian pastors and alleged child witches in Kinshasa, DRC." *On Knowing Humanity Journal: Anthropological Ethnography and Analysis Through the Eyes of Christian Faith* 4, no. 1 (2020): 1–51.

Robbins, Joel. "Beyond the Suffering Subject: Toward an Anthropology of the Good." *Journal of the Royal Anthropological Institute* 19, no. 3 (2013): 447–62.

Robbins, Joel. "Where Is the Good in the World?" In *Where is the Good in the World? Ethical Life between Social Theory and Philosophy*. Edited by David Henig, Anna Strhan, and Joel Robbins, 35–45. New York: Berghahn, 2022.

Sanneh, Lamin. *Translating the Message: The Missionary Impact on Culture*. Maryknoll, NY: Orbis, 2015.

Winter, Ralph D. "Seven Men, Four Eras." In *Frontiers in Mission*, edited by Ralph D. Winter, 308–16. Pasadena, CA: William Carey International University Press, 2008.

Wuthnow, Robert. *Boundless Faith: The Global Outreach of American Churches*. Berkeley: University of California Press, 2009.

Part One

Mission in Praise

As we contemplate God's global mission and our part in it, Scripture guides us to keep praise in the forefront of our minds. In Psalm 67:1–3, the psalmist prays: "May God be gracious to us and bless us and make his face to shine upon us, that your way may be known on earth, your saving power among all nations. Let the peoples praise you, O God; let all the peoples praise you!" In order to rightly engage in God's mission, praise and worship of God must be paramount. As John Piper observes, "worship ... is the fuel and goal of missions, [since] you can't commend what you don't cherish." Indeed, "Missionaries will never call out, 'Let the nations be glad!' if they cannot say from the heart, '*I rejoice* in the LORD ... *I will be glad and exult in you*, I will sing praise to your name, O Most High.'"[1]

As those participating in the mission of God, we begin with the end in mind, and this glorious end of global worship catalyzes praise in the here and now, which in turn guides and girds our gospel work. In this section, we explore the idea of ethnodoxology—a foretaste of heaven involving those from all nations, tribes, and tongues expressing their praise of God in ways that stem from and resonate with the artistic vernacular of their own culture rather than that of the missionary. We also look at trauma care through artistic expression that can bring healing and realign the sufferer with faith and hope in God. Finally, we are reminded that those engaged in mission work must remain aware of the reality of spiritual warfare and the need for a robust prayer life to stay connected to and empowered by Jesus, who "appeared ... to destroy the works of the devil" (1 John 3:8 ESV) and who makes this promise to those who seek to "make disciples of all nations" (Matt 28:19 ESV) as he commanded: "Behold, I am with you always, to the end of the age" (Matt 28:20 ESV).

---

1 Piper, *Nations Be Glad*, 35–36.

Chapter 1

The Future of Mission Is Local Worship

Robin P. Harris

My friend Sargylana was born in a remote region of Siberia—an area famous for its powerful shamans with deep roots in Sakha culture and animist religion. The Sakha people throughout the region have lived for countless generations in fear of these shamans, including their memorials and tombs. Sargylana is a soft-spoken, intelligent Sakha woman gifted in languages. She became a Christian while studying for a master's degree, and after graduating, was asked to help translate the Bible into Sakha.

Sargylana asked my friend Vera, a Ukrainian missionary, to bring some of her team to visit Sargylana's home village. Vera and her coworkers were the only believers who had ever visited this area other than Sargylana herself on her visits home.

Vera told me how when they arrived at Sargylana's village, her family greeted them with typical Sakha hospitality—a table groaning with all kinds of food. They insisted that the missionaries try the raw fish and the bear fat: "It's so good for you!" In common Siberian fashion, the missionaries sat around and sang after the meal. But the local Sakha had never heard these songs before—Christian songs in their own Sakha language. The family video-recorded the whole event.

Vera told me, "We could tell that their hearts had been touched when they began to flood us with questions." Sargylana's brother wanted to know how to repent, how to live after repentance, and if there was a need to stop feeding the spirit of the fire. Her father asked about creation and God as Creator. They both wanted to know about baptism: what is baptism, how do you do it, and what is its significance? The father and son eventually made a plan to visit the capital city, where Sargylana was living, to learn more.

Meanwhile, in a village not far from the capital, Sargylana's aunt Dunya got sick. Dunya called Sargylana and said, "I'm sick, so I'm coming into town and you will take me to the shaman." She had a very strong will and would not take no for an answer. Sargylana didn't want a conflict with her and came to Vera to pray together for wisdom in the situation. For several days they prayed. God answered in a very special way: the weekend Dunya was supposed to arrive ended up being the same time that Sargylana's father and brother were in town to find out more about God!

So Vera and Sargylana and her family met with Dunya and showed her the video they had just made in the village. The Christian songs in Sakha touched her very deeply. Sargylana also read to her from the New Testament in the Sakha language that she had been translating. Dunya's response to the singing and the joyful faces of the Christians was to change her mind—she didn't want to go to the shaman anymore. She said, "I love their songs—you will take me to *those* people!" Sargylana was delighted to do so!

They sang many songs, shared a meal together, and gave Dunya a New Testament and recordings of Christian songs. She left the place happy and couldn't stop talking about God. More than twenty-five years later, Dunya still talks with the Lord in simple heartfelt prayers, and every Sunday, Sargylana's brother reads the word of God to his family. Heart language Scripture as well as heart music and arts have led to lasting fruit in Sargylana's family. Vera told me after this experience in the mid-90s, "I am convinced that the music of the Sakha is a key that will open doors. I look forward to the day when a host of Sakha churches exist that will 'sing a new song' to God in their own heart music and their own heart language."

From Siberia to Columbia

These events happened early in our ministry in Siberia—shortly before we came to study at Columbia International University (CIU). It was one of many events that convinced me that *the future of mission is local worship*. Globalization and the ubiquitous marketing of Christian music have resulted in many evangelical Christian churches around the world singing and imitating the musical aesthetics of translated Hillsong and Bethel music. But local congregations still have other options. In fact, there is a growing movement that is emphasizing the importance of considering local forms of arts in worship. This new movement—some are calling it a discipline, or field of study—is *ethnodoxology*.

For me, missional engagement didn't start in Siberia. I was raised as a missionary kid in Alaska and went straight into cross-cultural service after graduating from college with a music major. For most of my life, however, my identity as a musician and my identity as a missionary were completely separate. It wasn't until we moved to Siberia in my 30s that I began to think about how music and cross-cultural service might have some overlap, providing a true vocation for me.

We lived as a family in northern Russia over a ten-year period and I continued to visit for the next fifteen years, until just before the pandemic. Our initial years were spent in Yakutsk, in a northern Siberian region of the Russian Federation, initially as cross-cultural consultants for a church planting team that was largely comprised of Belorussian and Ukrainian missionaries (like Vera), as well as a few American and Canadian families.

Yakutsk is the coldest inhabited city on earth. During the winter months at that time, it averaged about forty below zero. We went in the mid-1990s when Russians were coming to the Lord in droves. They wanted us to work with them to help start a bi-cultural church more appropriate for the minority Sakha population. We were asked to support and advise the Ukrainian and Belorussian church planting team as they accomplished that task.

The Soviet Union had marginalized Sakha arts, language, and culture, so after its dissolution, the traditional arts and music of the Sakha experienced a widespread renaissance. However, Russian forms of music and arts continued to dominate the expressive culture of the church. Since the music and culture reflected Russian aesthetics and values, few Sakha people were drawn to the church. Sakha people thought you had to take on Russian cultural values to become a Christian, so Sakha believers were reviled for being traitors to their people. The church planters encouraged the use of Sakha language, but initially, Sakha music, dance, poetry, storytelling, and visual arts were not used or encouraged. Unfortunately, we didn't have many artists or traditional musicians in the church. It's possible that artists didn't come because their gifts and talents in their own cultural styles weren't valued. Ultimately, it's difficult to say what caused this lack, but in the early years, the church didn't have musicians and artists who could create powerful expressions of local Sakha arts.

Even our mission agency didn't know what to think of my involvement in the indigenous arts. At one point, a coworker told me, "It would be better for your ministry if you weren't a musician." So I kept my head down and simply learned all I could. Besides, I didn't really know much about *how* to even encourage the use of local worship styles. I just knew that its lack was creating a barrier to the gospel for the Sakha people in our church.

My husband Bill also had many questions about how to approach church planting in this kind of cross-cultural context. So with all these questions swirling around in our heads and a furlough coming up, we decided to get some training in intercultural studies. After searching for a school we felt would best address our needs, we chose Columbia International University's graduate program in Intercultural Studies. That decision, as it turned out, was God's gift to us in many ways, but our CIU experience began with a huge disappointment.

We had chosen CIU partly because we had heard that the school had a specialist and some graduate courses related to ethnomusicology in missions. Upon our arrival, however, I learned that the professor for those courses, affectionately known as "Doc O," was on sabbatical. Deeply disappointed, I decided to make the best of the situation, joining Bill in a foundational course on Anthropology, taught by Dr. Robert Priest. That course truly changed my life. The first day of class, I came home bursting with enthusiasm and told Bill, "I love anthropology! I want to do the *whole degree* in Intercultural Studies (ICS)!"

In retrospect, it was God's gift to me that ethnomusicology classes were unavailable, as I would have been content to do those without the important foundation of a master's in ICS. After graduating from CIU, I was eventually able to get good ethnomusicology training at a different school, but starting with a foundation in ICS was just what I needed. As an added bonus, Robert Priest encouraged me to do some independent studies focusing on the music and arts of the Sakha, increasing my knowledge of our Siberian context in important ways, thereby setting a strong foundation for my eventual PhD.

After our time at CIU, we returned to Siberia and I began to apply what I had learned to our work with our church, leading to more stories like Vera's. Over time, applying principles of contextualization of the arts to our work with the Sakha really changed the way they saw their identity in Christ. They began to realize that they could use many of their cultural arts to glorify God and worship him.

In 2007, I helped to catalyze the formation of an Arts Fellowship led by local Sakha believers. They planned and prayed toward a big event that was a dream come true for them—the first Sakha New Song Festival. Because most non-Christians would not be willing to go to a church building for such an event, they rented a large hall near the center of town for the festival. They sent out invitations to their non-Christian friends and relatives from all over the region, hoping to fill the hall with curious seekers.

They prayed, planned, and prepared for months in anticipation of the festival, but just two days before the event, they received some bad news. Local authorities called the festival organizers and told them, "The hall will not be available for your event—the building will be closed that night." While the Arts Fellowship leaders were bitterly disappointed, it was not a huge surprise, because Protestant denominations were seen as sects, and Protestant Christians were increasingly feeling pressure from those in power. The religious freedoms so widespread after the fall of the Soviet Union were slowly being lost, a trajectory that continues to this day. The festival planners decided the only option they had was to hold it in the tiny church, so they announced that all church members who weren't participating should stay home so that there would be room for non-Christian guests. Then they gathered at the rented hall (now closed) on the evening of the festival, and stood in twenty degrees below zero temperatures to meet the attendees who were arriving, and point them to the path across the frozen pond to the church building about three hundred yards away. Of course, many were frightened off, not willing to visit a church building connected to a sect. Some, however, made the trek, and, in the end, the small church was packed—standing room only. For these non-Christian attendees, it was the first time they had seen expressions of Christianity that reflected Sakha language and culture. It was a powerful moment in the life of the Sakha church. I realized that night that the dream that I shared with Vera of Sakha believers "singing a new song" to God in their heart music and language had come true.

A few years later, at a large conference in central Siberia, on the inspiration from the festival in Yakutia, they held a "festival of the nations" with original songs and poetry from a large variety of ethnic groups. Our Sakha friends were amazed and encouraged to see that their example was stimulating indigenous groups from across Siberia to engage with their arts. In recent years, our Sakha friends have gone on to use their local music and arts in even more areas of their Christian worship. They are incorporating a traditional call-and-response circle dance called *ohuokai* for baptisms, weddings, and many other aspects of church life and family celebrations.

The church among the Sakha is finally growing. They are still figuring out what a Sakha Christ-follower looks like for their context, but many Sakha no longer feel like they have to abandon their cultural identity to engage with the life of the church there. Even the leader of the regional Council of Churches is Sakha, and a strong proponent of contextualization. In short, while it was my experience in Siberia that convinced me that local arts in worship are vitally important, it was my time at CIU—and especially the courses with Robert Priest—that helped me discover how to approach this issue and which gave me a love for anthropology and academics in general. My degree at CIU opened the door to a life-vocation of gathering, networking, and training others to use this new approach to the arts in mission—an approach now called ethnodoxology.

Ethno-What?

Ethno-dox-ology. It's a tough word to wrap your mouth around—in fact I've heard it pronounced as "ethno-toxicology"! What is this word—ethnodoxology—all about? Historically, there have been three approaches to arts in mission. These approaches should be viewed not as completely separate categories, but rather as a continuum.[1] Toward one end of the continuum is the *Bring It, Teach It* model, used by centuries of missionaries and church planters. In it, you bring what you know and what you love (what makes for good worship in your set of values), and teach it to others in cross-cultural contexts, assuming that it is probably the best way for them to worship as well.

But when you're working with people who have different cultural and artistic values than you, this can force you to teach them another artistic language to respond to God. Sometimes people will learn that artistic language, and they'll assume that you're right—it really is the right way to worship God. After generations of people learn to speak that artistic language, it can even become a heart language. This is one of the reasons why all over the world, people sing translated hymns and praise songs and think that they originated in their country.

On the other end of the spectrum is the *Find It, Encourage It* model of arts engagement, in which the person crossing cultural boundaries embraces incarnational principles for ministry: setting aside their own preferences, assuming a humble posture, and emptying themselves of their rights to worship in the ways that make them comfortable (Phil 2:5–8). They learn to value and appreciate the power of local ways of artistic expression, encouraging the use of those forms in worship and witness for the church.

Ethnodoxologists embrace this last approach, the *Find It, Encourage It* model of arts engagement rather than a *Bring It, Teach It* model. Between those two ends of the spectrum, lies a model we call *Building Bridges*. This approach also produces some great arts engagement, especially if you don't have enough time to learn much about the local arts that are available. It can include all kinds of relationship-building, kingdom-expanding creativity such as arts and trauma healing workshops, collaborative intercultural festivals, concerts, and exhibits; and cultural exchanges of all kinds.

---

1 Schrag and Harris, "Ethnodoxology's Time."

We also acknowledge that since these three approaches are on a continuum, and since arts are powerful connectors, good things have happened over the years using all three of these models.

Here is a concise definition of ethnodoxology developed by the Global Ethnodoxology Network: "Ethnodoxology is the interdisciplinary study of how Christians in every culture engage with God and the world through their own artistic expressions."[2] In ethnodoxology, it's not about using *my* performance specialty, or *my* arts in mission, but about helping people in communities to use *their* arts in responding to God's work in their lives—to respond in worship. You may be asking yourself, "Isn't all of this talk of arts and mission just for the artsy people to worry about?" Philip Graham Ryken points out that our creativity is a result of being created in the image of God. He says, "If the opening chapters of Genesis portray God as a creative artist, then it only stands to reason that the people he made in his image will also be artists. Art is an imaginative activity, and in the act of creating, we reflect the mind of our Maker."[3] So the biblical foundations of ethnodoxology are based in part on the creativity of God and his desire for us to respond to him in this aspect of the way he's created us—to embrace this gift of creativity, rather than marginalizing it. In the West, we sometimes have a distorted view of creativity, thinking that only professionals and the "talented" have the right to be called creative. We need to recover a biblical theology of the arts that sees God's people as full of (often untapped) creativity.

Ethnodoxology Values for Contemporary Mission

In 2003, at the apex of my struggles for finding like-minded people for mutual support in the fledgling field of ethnodoxology, I co-founded a network that is known today as the Global Ethnodoxology Network (GEN). One of the projects we launched as we approached our twentieth anniversary in 2023 was the creation of a statement of core values for ethnodoxologists.[4] I won't review all of them in this chapter, but I'd like to highlight a few that help to explain what we mean by *local* when we talk about local worship.

---

2 In addition to this official definition at the GEN website, there are also other good definitions listed. See also the explanatory video, produced by OM's Inspiro Arts Alliance, "What Is Ethnodoxology?"

3 Ryken, "Art for God's Sake," 24.

4 "Core Values." I am grateful for the work of my colleagues Jean Kidula, James Krabill, and Brian Schrag for their outstanding work on the foundational draft of these value statements. This section draws freely from that document (with permission).

But first, I'll start with a story about an experience I had in southern Siberia that illustrates what local worship is *not*. In 2008, Bill and I took a group of ethnodoxologists to the Republic of Tuva, a southern Siberian region of the Russian Federation, right next to Mongolia. Tuva and Mongolia are both well-known for throat-singing, an unusual form of vocal production that has fascinated ethnomusicologists for decades.[5] The evangelical churches in Tuva had both Russian and Tuvan believers in them, but just as we had experienced in Yakutsk, most of the worship of the church was expressed in either Russian or Western styles of music and arts. We were there to encourage them in their use of Tuvan styles of music and arts in worship. We brought high-quality recording equipment and recorded them singing and playing local instruments as well as some of the Tuvan songs they had recently written.

At one church in particular, I met with the Tuvans on the worship team and asked them about the music and arts expressions of their church. They told me that the worship team met on Saturday afternoons at three to practice for church the next day. They said, "Our Russian worship leader rehearses with us for at least three hours to help us learn translated Hillsongs for the service. Sometimes even after three or four hours, we can't do a good enough job to make the leader happy. So many times on the next day the worship leader will cut a song right before church, telling us that even after all that practice, it's not good enough. We try very hard to get it right, but Hillsongs are difficult! The whole thing is very disheartening for us."

That's an example of *not* using local expressions in worship. But how does ethnodoxology describe its core values for fostering local worship?

Christian Worship: Celebrating the Stunning Variety of Christian Worship Patterns in the Global Church

During CIU's one hundredth anniversary celebration, we experienced that "stunning variety" by worshipping with the world worship band IziBongo.[6] For many, it was a glorious window on what worship in heaven might be like, and the band rejoiced that CIU invited them to lead multicultural worship for a conference on the Future of Mission.[7] Groups like IziBongo

---

5   We also spent time with a Tuvan singing group that performs all over the world (Alash). This video clip features them and explains Tuvan throat singing: Didge Project, "Tuvan Throat Singing Masters: Alash Ensemble," June 12, 2018, YouTube video, 3:24.

6   According to the group's website, "IziBongo refers to 'praises intoned in honor of a person.' This genre of praise poetry comes from the Zulu people of South Africa."

7   See CIU's conference recap video that features IziBongo: "Future of Global Mission Conference | Highlights 2022."

are multiplying around the world as Christians catch a vision for the importance of learning about the variety of worship styles in the body of Christ. These groups help us develop that important ethnodoxological skill of setting aside what's comfortable and learning to join in with artistic languages that challenge us and stretch us, singing and worshipping in solidarity with brothers and sisters around the world.

Experiencing global worship styles is important because the global church exhibits an amazing variety of worship patterns. We believe that this variety demonstrates the vastness of God's creativity and the diversity of the body of Christ—a diversity we believe is already visible, but will be celebrated into eternity.

We see in passages like Revelation 7:9 that God will be worshiped by *panta ta ethne*—every nation, tribe, people, and language. Revelation 21:26 describes the heavenly city and the worship there as involving the bringing of the "glory and honor of the nations"—or "the glorious *treasures* of the nations" (CEV) into the city. Since we know from John 4:23, 24 that what God wants from humankind is our heartfelt worship, it's likely that the treasures of the nations include their unique expressions of heart worship.[8] Ethnodoxologists prepare for that great day by celebrating that diversity and creativity in the global body of Christ as we worship our great God.

Human Agency: Respecting the Right and Capacity of People to Shape their Own Artistic Realities

Although we value the diversity of human creativity in worship, this particular value makes it clear that we don't stipulate what kinds of creativity people are allowed to express. We encourage them to make their own decisions, based on the Holy Spirit's work in their lives and their response to the word of God. In doing this, we draw from the principles of Romans 14 about not judging one another for choices in cultural matters. This goes against our natural desire to impose our own cultural values on others, but once again, we are reminded of Philippians 2:3, 4: "in humility value others above yourselves, not looking to your own interests but each of you to the interests of the others."

---

8 Krabill et al. 2013. In Isaiah 60 we see a prophecy in which the nations bring their *wealth* and their *worship* to a triumphant king in his city: "Nations will come to your light, and kings to the brightness of your dawn (v. 3) ... to you the riches of the nations will come (v. 5) ... bearing gold and incense and proclaiming the praise of the Lord (v. 6). This image—of homage (wealth and worship) brought to a ruler and his city by the nations—is reflected in Rev 21: 22–26.

Too often, outsiders have made decisions for communities, rather than trusting the work of the Holy Spirit in local decisions regarding which kinds of artistic forms to employ in their witness and worship. This is true not only in cross-cultural situations, but even in micro-cultural contexts in our own home culture. Let's resist the temptation to think we know what kinds of artistic expression people should use to worship the Lord.

Locally-grounded Methods: Amplifying Local Agency and Creativity

This value is demonstrated by our use of participatory methods, not doing things *for* local people but rather *with* them. In other words, local voices shape the outcomes of the projects we do in communities. Toward that end, ethnodoxologists have developed some insightful, practical methods for arts contextualization. These methods are being taught in everything from workshops in various languages[9] to courses at the BA, MA, and PhD levels.[10] This training can teach us to raise questions and open conversations that help people think more deeply about their local artistic resources and how they might engage them.

But in all these methods, agency—the right and responsibility to make decisions—lies with local faith communities as they seek wisdom from God. I'd encourage you to consider your arts ministry, or ministries that you know, and ponder the degree to which leaders are valuing the voice of local communities in these difficult issues of localization and contextualization.

Historical Awareness: Situating Goals and Activities within Global, Regional, and Local Histories

The GEN core values affirm that:

> We recognize the complex and constantly changing nature of every individual's and community's artistry and worship practices, including our own. Because Euro-American art forms have largely accompanied the spread of Christianity in recent centuries, local artistic traditions—especially those of ethnolinguistic minorities—often remain outside the church. Ethnodoxology seeks to redress this imbalance by retaining a robust engagement with representatives of local, older, often rural artistic histories. We also celebrate urban multicultural, multiartistic identities and creativity that mark more and more Christian communities.[11]

---

9   Two workshop options developed by the GEN are "Arts for a Better Future" and "Introduction to Ethnodoxology."

10   See for example, the intensive courses offered by the Center for Excellence in World Arts.

11   "Core Values," *Global Ethnodoxology Network*.

For both urban and rural groups—really for all people—we seek to support them as they create their own unique worship expressions (Ps 33:3; Col 3:16).

For example, Joy Kim, a GEN board member, used ethnodoxology methods for her master's project in a multicultural urban refugee community near Atlanta. Her thesis[12] describing that project provides an amazing example of ethnodoxology methods, and her ongoing ministry with Proskuneo Ministries in that community is producing intercultural, multilingual expressions of a broad variety of arts in worship: movement, American Sign Language, hospitality and ethnic cuisine, crafts, poetry, proverbs, cultural forms of greeting and structuring their gatherings, as well as many multi-generational activities that include everyone, from the children to the elders.[13] This multiethnic worshipping community perfectly illustrates the connection between hospitality and worship as described by Ed Smither, who points out that "strangers, both believers in Christ and nonbelievers bear the image of God and are worthy of welcome, and the ministry of welcome is ultimately an act of worship to our Lord."[14]

In short, ethnodoxologists respond to historical realities not by insisting that local arts *only* include "traditional" arts (although in many cases that is an important part of the response), but that they include at least *some* arts that are created by that community rather than only borrowing from other communities. The worship arts they create, and their life as a community, is marked by expressions that uniquely reflect their varied backgrounds and the generational diversity of the group.

Local Worship and the Future of Mission

Unfortunately, I have observed that in many mission agencies, artists and musicians are marginalized. Matt Taylor, a missionary with significant artistic gifts, recently told me that he grew up in an environment where pursuing arts as a career was not looked fondly upon. He wrote: "I became drawn to church planting and foreign missions. For many years after, I thought that by choosing to be a missionary, I was laying my arts interests at Jesus's feet and considering it an offering to be burned up, turned to ash, and rendered useless." It wasn't until Matt discovered ethnodoxology that he realized that God valued this part of his identity. He writes, "God is using this [ethnodoxology] training to not only equip me, but so

---

12 Kim, "Diaspora Musicians."
13 Learn more about Proskuneo Ministries at their website, https://proskuneo.org/.
14 Smither, *Mission as Hospitality*, 120.

many others. And, in turn, I am training and equipping cross-cultural church planters with much of the insight I have gained."[15]

Lausanne's "Cape Town Commitment" outlines one more reason why local arts are important: "Artists at their best are truth-tellers and so the arts constitute one important way in which we can speak the truth of the gospel ... We long to see the church in all cultures energetically engaging the arts as a context for mission."[16] If we eliminate local agency in the arts expression of the church, we eliminate one of the most powerful tools we have for speaking the truth of the gospel.

In summary, ethnodoxology affirms that God has given to all cultures *all* they need in music and the arts for the life, worship, and ministry of the church. If you're wondering if anyone really does this, the answer is yes! The list of organizations with positions for ethnodoxologists is growing.[17] The Global Ethnodoxology Network is working to connect these organizations and provides training and resources for fostering local worship globally. I believe that the future of mission includes embracing this vision for ethnodoxology approaches, and that it will become the *normal way of doing arts in mission.*

---

15 Personal correspondence, July 9, 2021. See Matt Taylor's art on his Facebook page, Matt Taylor Arts, and his study program in World Arts at the Center for Excellence in World Arts.

16 "Cape Town Commitment," 61.

17 At of the beginning of 2023, organizations with positions for ethnodoxologists include the following: Africa Inland Mission (AIM), Artists in Christian Testimony (ACT), OM (Inspiro Arts Alliance), Lutheran Bible Translators, Pioneer Bible Translators, Pioneers, Mission to the World, Music in World Cultures (MIWC), SIL International, SIM, To Every Tribe, WEC (Arts Release), and Wycliffe Bible Translators.

Bibliography

"Core Values." *Global Ethnodoxology Network* (blog). Accessed January 14, 2023. https://www.worldofworship.org/core-values/.

Didge Project. "Tuvan Throat Singing Masters: Alash Ensemble." June 12, 2018. YouTube video, 3:24. https://youtu.be/ufG9S6X8FDM.

"Future of Global Mission Conference | Highlights 2022." January 27, 2023. YouTube video 4:02. https://www.youtube.com/watch?v=qR3-VGKozAk.

"IziBongo." World-Wide-Worship. http://www.ethnodoxology.org/izibongo/.

Kim, Joy. "Diaspora Musicians and Creative Collaboration in a Multicultural Community: A Case Study in Ethnodoxology." MA thesis, Dallas International University, 2018. https://diu.edu/documents/theses/Kim_Joy-thesis.pdf.

Krabill, James R., Frank Fortunato, Robin P. Harris, and Brian Schrag. *Worship and Mission for the Global Church: An Ethnodoxology Handbook*. Pasadena, CA: William Carey Publishing, 2013. https://www.worldofworship.org/ethnodoxology-handbook-manual/.

Ryken, Philip Graham. *Art for God's Sake: A Call to Recover the Arts*. Phillipsburg, NJ: P&R Publishing, 2006.

Schrag, Brian, and Robin Harris. "Ethnodoxology's Time Is Here: How Engaging Local Artists Can Expand God's Kingdom." *Lausanne Global Analysis* 3, no. 1: (2014). https://conversation.lausanne.org/resources/detail/13404/.

Smither, Edward L. *Mission as Hospitality: Imitating the Hospitable God in Mission*. Eugene, OR: Cascade, 2021.

"The Cape Town Commitment: A Confession of Faith and a Call to Action." Lausanne Library. Accessed January 14, 2023. https://lausanne.org/wp-content/uploads/2021/10/The-Cape-Town-Commitment-%E2%80%93-Pages-20-09-2021.pdf.

"What Is Ethnodoxology?" *Global Ethnodoxology Network* (blog). https://www.worldofworship.org/what-is-ethnodoxology/.

"What Is Ethnodoxology?" June 8, 2021. YouTube video. https://www.youtube.com/watch?v=rHv61zK_gp4.

Chapter 2

Trauma Care and the Arts in Mission

Wendy Atkins

One summer I was traveling on the back of a motorbike in the Ituri Rain Forest in the Democratic Republic of Congo. Our team of several pastors and myself were heading one hundred kilometers northwest from our homes in Banda to spend the weekend celebrating the ordination of two pastors. My chauffeur, the director of the French Bible Institute in Banda where I teach, had traveled this road many times. When we came to a heavily wooded area of the road, he began talking, telling me how he and another pastor had been stopped at that spot by rebel forces. He recounted the details of the guns the rebels carried, their uniforms, and how they were herded off the road into the forest, the rebels stripping them of all their clothing. There, they were forced to shell peanuts for several hours. After looting their goods—telephones, money, food, and other valuables—the rebels released them. Several years after this event took place, the traumatic memories were still vivid. His trauma story was still fresh. He shared all the details with me as we rode along. By telling his trauma story, he made another step towards healing from that experience.

The Importance of Trauma Care through the Arts

The experience of this pastor is unfortunately a common event in much of the world today. Even a quick glance at current events reveals that many populations suffer from war, rebel activity, natural disasters, and other major trauma-inducing events. In addition to these sources of trauma, many face gun violence, political divisions and unrest, sexual harassment, and divorce. Trauma occurs as the result of a one-time or prolonged series of events that overwhelm a person's ability to cope; it is an internal response "as a result of an overwhelmingly negative event or series of events."[1] Trauma affects the emotions, the body, and the mind, producing altered emotional responses,

---
1 Saurman et al., "Trauma Healing Process," 16.

altered thinking, and altered physical reactions. Noted psychologist and trauma specialist, Diane Langberg, says that trauma "swallows up and destroys normal human ways of living."[2]

A traumatized person finds it difficult to listen and reason well. No matter how wonderful the message, trauma affects the brain, causing diminished reception and understanding of the information being shared. The prevalence of trauma in the world today makes it difficult for people to respond to the good news of Christ in life-changing ways. Caring for the traumatized, helping them share their difficult experiences to find release from their traumatic memories, creates opportunities for enhanced reception of the gospel message. When a traumatized person expresses himself or herself through activities involving music, movement, visual arts, drama, and written expression such as poetry or storytelling, avenues develop allowing for the expression of his trauma story, paving the way for better understanding of the gospel.

Biblical Foundations

Christ's example compels us to reach out to those hurting from traumatic incidents. Consider the boy the disciples were not able to help (Matt 17:14–18), the Gerasene Demoniac (Mark 5:1–13), the woman suffering from hemorrhages for twelve years (Luke 8:43–48), and the Samaritan woman at the well (John 4:7–26). These are just a few of the traumatized people for whom Jesus cared. Each of these individuals was overwhelmed by circumstances and unable to function normally in daily life. Jesus met each one in their place of pain, bringing physical, emotional, and spiritual relief.

Several New Testament references urge us to reach out to those dealing with trauma, challenging us to actually shed tears with those who cry (Rom 12:15), suffer with those who suffer (1 Cor 12:26), and to remember those who are overwhelmed by their circumstances (Heb 13:3). The message of the gospel proclaims freedom from physical, mental, emotional, and spiritual trauma. That message of freedom provides the only true hope for a traumatized person to find complete wholeness and well-being. In *Suffering and the Heart of God*, Langberg writes this about the role of the church in trauma healing:

> Sadly, the body of Christ has often failed to see trauma as a place of service. If we survey the extensive natural disasters in our time—earthquakes, hurricanes, and tsunamis—and combine those victims with human atrocities—the violent inner cities, wars, genocides, trafficking, rapes, and child abuse—we

---

2 Langberg, "Trauma as a Place," 2.

would have a staggering number. I think a look at suffering humanity would lead to the realization that trauma is perhaps the greatest mission field of the twenty-first century.[3]

As we acknowledge the effects of trauma on so many in the world, we as the church must recognize the responsibility and opportunity to minister the healing power of Christ to the hurting.

The Role of the Arts in Trauma Care

The word of God, as well as the mandate of the church to embody Christ's example, compels us to engage with trauma victims by listening to their stories. By sharing a trauma story, the speaker begins to find release from the emotional, physical, mental, and spiritual effects of trauma. They become ready to listen to the message of Jesus Christ as Comforter and Healer as the emotions, physical sensations, and thoughts that block perception find means of expression.

Why use art forms in this process? Research shows that traumatic experiences "are encoded in the limbic system and the right hemisphere of the brain," the area governing creative expression.[4] The sights, smells, sounds, sensations, and emotions associated with the experience are held in the right hemisphere, disrupting brain integration.[5] Using the arts to express what one experienced in a traumatic situation emphasizes right-brain functions but also accesses the whole brain. Allowing for artistic expression of these sensations helps brain integration as the right hemisphere functions of the brain facilitate creation and the left hemisphere functions guide cognitive engagement.

The role of the arts in facilitating the telling of a trauma story is especially important when verbalizing the experience becomes difficult.[6] In some trauma cases, the Broca's area of the brain, an area that controls aspects of speech, ceases to function, blocking speech.[7] Along with this inability to verbalize a trauma story, it is important to note that memories of trauma sometimes do not even have linguistic components. These memories are stored in the brain in images and sensations. Sharing these sensations happens more easily when communicated through sensory

---

3 Langberg, *Suffering and the Heart*, 8.
4 van der Kolk, *Body Keeps the Score*, quoted in Malchiodi, *Trauma and Expressive Arts*, 66.
5 Malchiodi, *Trauma and Expressive Arts*, 66.
6 Malchiodi, 65.
7 Newhouse, "Vets Experiencing Trauma."

experiences rather than through words.[8] Creating a visual representation of the emotions associated with the traumatic experience using colored markers, releasing the physical pain stored in the body through movement, or humming an improvised melody while reflecting on the emotions connected with one's trauma all serve as non-verbal expressions of the sensations related to a trauma experience. Each artistic expression accesses functions of the right hemisphere of the brain to enhance integration with the left hemisphere, promoting horizontal integration.[9]

Expressing one's trauma through the arts also encourages vertical integration of the brain. Vertical integration involves the brainstem or lower brain, the limbic system or middle brain, and the cortex or upper brain. As trauma strikes, the sights, sounds, smells, and other sensations involved in the traumatic event first invade the limbic system that analyzes the flood of information. The brainstem then sends a message to the body. Milliseconds later, cognitive reasoning attempts to sort out the sensations, sending a message back to the brainstem that determines whether to attack the cause of the trauma, run away from it, or freeze in fear. When trauma strikes, these three areas of the brain do not necessarily function normally.[10] Engaging with the arts as a means of expressing a trauma memory involves the lower, middle, and upper brain as the body, emotions, and thoughts are involved in the creation of the art form. As artistic expression facilitates the sharing of aspects of the trauma experienced, right hemisphere and left hemisphere brain functions are activated. Lower, middle, and upper brain functions also engage, leading towards whole-brain integration. The arts facilitate the process of this integration as the individual expresses his hurt and pain through an artistic creation then shares "the emotions and feelings connected with the actual creation as well as the creative process."[11]

The arts provide ways for traumatized people to express their stories in ways that engage the whole being, often stimulating verbalization of the trauma experienced. During a workshop focusing on the principles of trauma healing, participants were asked to use various visual art supplies to represent the feelings they experienced during a time when they felt overwhelmed. One woman placed three blobs of different colored modeling

---

8   "101 Trauma-informed Art."
9   Malchiodi, *Trauma and Expressive Arts*, 66.
10 Siegle, "Minding the Brain."
11 Saurman et al., "Trauma Healing Process," 23.

clay on a large sheet of colored construction paper. After allowing time to create as well as share their creations and the experience of creating them with people sitting near them, I asked if anyone wanted to share with the large group. This woman immediately jumped up, holding her paper for all to see.

> I am not going to tell you what these blobs of clay represent. But after molding them and placing them on this paper, I was able to share with the person sitting next to me a traumatic event that took place in my life over twenty years ago. This is the first time I ever felt ready to share with anyone the feelings, sensations, and thoughts I still have as a result of that experience. Now that I have shared them, I feel free of the physical, mental, and spiritual weight I have been carrying ever since that time.

It is important to note that this woman was comfortable using modeling clay to express her experience because her cultural background included working with modeling clay from the time she was a child. Clay served as a familiar artistic medium with which she could freely create. Using local art forms increases the efficacy of engaging with the arts in trauma care. Familiar, local art forms allow for free, unhindered expression of a trauma story. Using art forms not inherent within the culture adds barriers to expression as the focus then becomes on learning how to perform or create with the unfamiliar art form and not on telling the trauma story. Just as communicating in a local language facilitates the understanding of the message, engaging with local art forms to tell a trauma story allows for deeper, fuller expression of that experience.

When facilitating a trauma healing group with women at a Bible school in central Africa, I asked the students to think about a traumatic time in their lives. I then challenged them to go outside to find something in nature—leaves, sticks, rocks, flowers—they could use to represent their pain. One woman returned with five small stones. As she shared, she presented each stone one by one, explaining five sources of her trauma. Her first husband had beaten her. His family had slandered her. Her friends had treated her as an outcast. She fell sick with a strange pain in her jaw. Neighbors stole things from her. As she placed each stone on the table, she shared different aspects of her trauma story. When she finished, she said that she felt peace in her heart. Her artistic expression was nothing elaborate that required outside materials. She used what was available to express her emotional pain, engaging her emotions, body, and mind in the telling of her trauma story.

Other aspects of engaging with local arts enhance trauma care as well. Singing a song, arranging photos into a collage, creating a series of movements to music, or carving locally available wood encourages self-regulation and produces a sense of calmness. As people represent their traumatic feelings and thoughts through specific artistic efforts resulting in a visible representation, those feelings and thoughts become tangible, as they did for the woman using modeling clay at the workshop. Efforts to represent the trauma in an artistic form of expression become a means of dealing with the effects of the trauma, allowing the individual to gain a sense of order and control over what he experienced, enhancing the individual's ability to gain an understanding of the traumatic event.[12] Engaging with an artistic form as a way of communicating the sensations and thoughts connected to a traumatic experience also has "a unique role in restoring a sense of vitality and joy in traumatized individuals."[13]

Exploring and expressing trauma stories through artistic forms of communication facilitate the healing process. But simply telling the story is not enough. As trauma stories are shared, we find ways to encourage those who are hurting to look to Jesus as the ultimate Healer. He is the one who meets us in our overwhelming, traumatic situations. He is the one who provides healing for our emotions, bodies, minds, and souls. That is the message of hope we bring to those who are hurting. We do not belittle the telling of their trauma stories, but as people share, and become ready to listen, we emphasize that God is there to help them in their struggles. When traumatized people engage with a local artistic form as a means of expressing their emotions, feelings, and thoughts, they are more fully able to acknowledge, and share their pain, finding healing from traumatic experiences and renewed faith in God as he helps them to do so.

---

12 Malchiodi, *Trauma and Expressive Arts*, 25–26.
13 Malchiodi, 32.

Bibliography

Langberg, Diane. *Suffering and the Heart of God: How Trauma Destroys and Christ Restores*. Greensboro, NC: New Growth Press, 2015.

Langberg, Diane. "Trauma as a Place of Service." National Church Leaders Summit, Bible House, NYC, 2011.

Malchiodi, Cathy A. *Trauma and Expressive Arts Therapy: Brain, Body, & Imagination in the Healing Process*. New York: Guilford Press, 2020.

Newhouse, Eric. "Vets Experiencing Trauma Can't Respond to Reason: Traumatized brains are ruled by emotion, not logic." *Psychology Today*, December 17, 2015. https://www.psychologytoday.com/us/blog/invisible-wounds/201512/vets-experiencing-trauma-cant-respond-reason.

Saurman, Mary Beth, Todd Saurman, Wendy Atkins, and Beth Randolph. *Arts in the Trauma Healing Process*. Pre-published Manual, 2021.

Siegel, Daniel. "Minding the Brain." Psychalive. Accessed January 26, 2021. https://www.psychalive.org/minding-the-brain-by-daniel-siegel-m-d-2/.

Trauma-Informed Practices & Expressive Arts Therapy Institute. "101 Trauma-Informed Art Therapy." Accessed October 15, 2015. https://www.trauma-informedpractice.com/.

van der Kolk, Bessel A. *The Body Keeps the Score*. New York: Penguin, 2014.

Further Reading

"Arts and Trauma Healing." Dallas International University. Accessed January 15, 2023. www.diu.edu/ath.

Barker, Paul A., ed. *Tackling Trauma: Global, Biblical, and Pastoral Perspectives*. Carlisle, UK: Langham, 2019.

Hill, Harriet, Margaret Hill, Richard Bagge, and Pat Miersma. *Healing the Wounds of Trauma: How the Church Can Help*. New York: American Bible Society, 2016.

Chapter 3

Prayer and Spiritual Warfare in Global Mission

David Cashin and Victor H. Cuartas

Introduction

This chapter aims to provide a biblical and strategic perspective of prayer and spiritual warfare in global mission. The reader will be equipped with biblical and practical strategies for developing a lifestyle of prayer and spiritual warfare within their outreach. The first part of the chapter will describe the importance of prayer and spiritual warfare, highlighting important Scriptures and biblical principles. The second part will focus on stories and narratives from different ministry contexts. Finally, the authors provide a list of sources for further study.

Importance of Prayer and Spiritual Warfare in Global Mission

When we think about the Great Commission and global mission (Matt 28:18–20), we see the clash of two kingdoms, the kingdom of light and the kingdom of darkness (John 1:5; 2 Cor 4:6). Forty-two percent of the world's people groups still need access to the gospel, and the enemy is actively working to prevent it. The spiritual resistance is real. Thus, as followers of Christ who are sent daily to proclaim the good news of the gospel locally and globally, we must pray, fast, and ask the Holy Spirit to give us wisdom and discernment to overcome Satan. We need to be aware of the strategies of the enemy. This reality for believers is not a playground but a battleground. The ultimate goal of the enemy is to destroy our trust and confidence in God.

David Jeremiah writes, "Satan is none too happy about what God has accomplished in Christ. His main goal is to destroy the faith of Christians by getting them to doubt God's goodness, love, forgiveness, protection, provision, and promises. When Satan creates difficult circumstances in our lives, it is not just to inflict pain; it is for the purpose of destroying our trust in God."[1] However, our victory is in Christ Jesus. The Apostle Paul adds, "When he had disarmed the rulers and authorities, He made a public display of them, having triumphed over them through him" (Col 2:15 NASB). No matter what the enemy tries to throw our way, trust that the battle is already won in Jesus's name. This truth is a powerful reassurance as we embark on spiritual warfare while we continue to proclaim the great news of salvation and redemption.

Different Approaches to Spiritual Warfare

There are different approaches to spiritual warfare. In one approach, the tendency is to consider that everything negative is from the devil. The main focus in this approach is on the enemy with little focus on God or his promises. Another approach, especially common in the Western world, is to think that the devil is a myth that does not exist. This view is dangerous because it opens the doors to the enemy's attacks (1 Pet 5:8–10 NASB). He is the father of lies (John 8:44 NASB), and his first strategy is to make himself look larger than he is. His second strategy is to convince people that he does not exist. We must recognize the fact that Satan is real and came "to steal, kill, and destroy" (John 10:10a NASB). The great news for us is that Jesus came so that we would "have life and have it abundantly" (John 10:10b NASB). We need to avoid these extremes to have a balanced, biblical approach.

As followers of Christ, we need a biblical approach regarding the authenticity of spiritual warfare. We must recognize that the enemy is real and that we are in a constant spiritual battle. Believers can overcome the enemy through the power of the Holy Spirit and God's promises in the Scriptures. God has provided everything that we need to overcome the enemy. Satan has already been defeated by Christ. We are the only army that can go to battle already knowing the outcome. We are victorious in Christ Jesus (1 Cor 15:57 NASB).

Because God's promises have power, our focus needs to be on God and the Scriptures. First, we need to know and understand who God is and reflect on his attributes. Second, it is important to know and realize who we are in him: our identity and position are secure in him. He knows our limitations and the strategies the enemy uses against us. We are encouraged to acknowledge the enemy and beware of his schemes (Eph 6:11 NASB). The more we align our lives with God's mission, the more resistance we

---

[1] David Jeremiah, *Answers to Questions*, 2–3.

should expect from the enemy. God wants to reveal himself to all his creation. It is paramount to rely daily on the guidance and power of the Holy Spirit.

Biblical Foundations of Prayer and Spiritual Warfare

First, Paul admonishes us about the need to recognize the nature of warfare and the spiritual weapons that are needed.

> For though we walk in the flesh, we do not wage battle according to the flesh, for the weapons of our warfare are not of the flesh, but divinely powerful for the destruction of fortresses. We are destroying arguments and all arrogance raised against the knowledge of God, and we are taking every thought captive to the obedience of Christ. (2 Cor 10:3–5 NASB)

Second, we need to totally surrender and submit to God. James wrote, "Submit therefore to God. Resist the devil and he will flee from you. Come close to God and he will come close to you. Cleanse your hands, you sinners; and purify your hearts, you double-minded" (Jas 4:7–8 NASB).

Third, God has provided a spiritual armor to defeat the enemy. In Paul's letter to the Ephesians, we find the spiritual armor that God provided to overcome Satan (Eph 6:10–20 NASB). Our strength is in the Lord, not in our own efforts or knowledge (v. 10). There is an emphasis on "putting on the armor of God" (vv. 11, 13). This is something that we need to do daily by faith. The passage also emphasizes "standing firm" (vv. 11, 13, 14), and Paul urges the believers to "be alert" (v. 18). He warns believers to "stand firm" against the schemes of the devil and "to resist" in the evil day (vv. 11, 13). Paul goes on to describe the armor of God through the following images:

> Stand firm, therefore, having belted your waist with truth, and having put on the breastplate of righteousness, and having strapped on your feet the preparation of the gospel of peace; in addition to all, taking up the shield of faith with which you will be able to extinguish all the flaming arrows of the evil one. And take the helmet of salvation, and the sword of the Spirit, which is the word of God. With every prayer and request, pray at all times in the Spirit, and with this in view, be alert with all perseverance and every request for all the saints. (Eph 6:14–18 NASB)

Notice that prayer and intercession are vital elements of the armor of God. Paul also highlights his need for prayer in order to proclaim the gospel with boldness (Eph 6:19–20 NASB).

Spiritual Warfare Illustrated

Scripture, as we have seen, provides a rich narrative of the reality of spiritual warfare. Western secular society has relegated this reality to the realm of superstition, and that rationalistic tendency often influences Western Christians. Thankfully there is a Majority World of experience that can help missionaries to perceive the reality of the demonic and to learn how to deal with it. Since the majority of missionaries today come from the Global South, they have much to teach those from the Global North on this topic.

The following three stories, from my (David) own life and the lives of some of my closest associates, illustrate something of that learning process. I went overseas as a missionary in 1980, and though I gave lip service to the reality of a spiritual world, I had very little experience or expectations. My first story is very positive in that it showed me how God was engaged in sharing the gospel with Muslims. The task is not about me; it is about our sovereign Lord and how he intervenes on our behalf.

God Speaks through Dreams

I had started a small church planting station in a town (we'll call it, *K*) in a Muslim nation. I invited Muslims that I met to the small room I rented for Bible studies and monthly all-night meetings. One day as I was engaged in Bible study with several Muslims, a gentleman named Seyyid came into the room. I had never seen him before, which made me a little suspicious. He sat down on the bamboo mat next to me, looked me square in the eye, and said, "What does Matthew 1:21 say?" I had never had a Muslim ask me that before, so I asked him why he wanted to know. "Well," he said, "Jesus told me to ask you!" So how did Jesus do that? The previous night had been the Laylat al-Qadr celebration, where Muslims stay up all night praying to ensure God's blessing on their fate for the coming year. There is one condition to this vigil: you must not fall asleep, or it is "no soup for you!" Seyyid's spirit was willing, but his flesh was weak, and he fell asleep in the middle of the night.

As Seyyid slept, he had a dream. First, he met two already deceased spiritual figures from his past, and he took the opportunity to ask them the most important questions a Muslim can ask—"What is the way of salvation? And how can I know if God will accept my deeds?" Because salvation in Islam is based on one's deeds, both men sadly shook their heads and said they did not know. But both also indicated that another man would come who might answer the question. Then a third man appeared in his dream.

I don't know how Muslim friends recognize him, but they always do. It was the Lord Jesus Christ. Seyyid asked the same question, and Jesus said, "I will show you the way of salvation. But first, you must go to the missionary in K and ask him what Matthew 1:21 says." Seyyid had never seen a Bible; he had no idea what Matthew 1:21 referred to. So I opened the passage for him where the angel is speaking to Joseph and says to him, "You shall name him Jesus, for he will save his people from their sins." Starting from that passage, I shared the gospel, and Seyyid came to faith in Christ. He was the only Muslim I have ever known to believe in Christ the same day he first heard the gospel.

This event had very little to do with me other than that I was where I was supposed to be. It not only opened my eyes to the reality that God can speak today through dreams, but it also demonstrated to me that *God* is doing the work of drawing people to himself. You and I are merely partners with him in that process.

The Reality of Spiritual Attacks

The next story was shared by a gentleman who discipled me for a number of years for ministry in the Muslim world. Don was and is a very deeply devoted Christian, effective evangelist, and missionary to Muslims. Perhaps that is why his experience is all the more startling.

Don was a WWII veteran who had been discipled through the Navigators and was serving as a pastor when God called him to ministry in the Muslim world. After he finished his first year of language study, he was placed in a town to serve in theological education. He and his family rented a house there.

Immediately upon their moving into this new home, Don began wrestling with depression. This experience was totally unusual for him. He had hardly been depressed a day in his life. Yet, suddenly, his world went black. He found Bible study and prayer increasingly impossible. His mind became consumed with suicidal thoughts. When he approached his mission agency about the problem, they responded from a cessationist point of view—that spiritual warfare and the miraculous was limited to biblical times. They offered counsel and medication but the problem only got worse.

After getting no help from his mission organization, Don decided to consult some local Pentecostal pastors to see if they might have a solution. They gathered at Don's house, and after listening to Don's problems, they said, "You have been placed under a curse by local witches and warlocks." Don was initially in disbelief, not knowing that witchcraft and sorcery are common among Muslims, and were even recorded in the life of Muhammad. They said it was likely that some kind of fetish had been buried near the house and that it was probably situated near the corners of the house foundations. They began to dig and found, astonishingly, not one but four fetishes had been buried around the house. The fetishes were skeletal heads of goats whose horns had been festooned with *thabij*, amulets that contained verses of cursing *rukya* (incantational magic) from the Qur'an. They instructed Don to burn the goat's heads and *thabij* in an incinerator and to pray and cleanse the house, dedicating it to the Lord. Overnight, Don's depression vanished.

What does this event teach us? First, spiritual attacks with physiological consequences are possible and a mature believer in Christ can be affected. The spirit world and spiritual attacks are real. Second, the Western Christian world can be guilty of its own syncretism, interpreting the world through the rationalistic lens of the Enlightenment. All phenoma can be explained physiologically or psychologically. Some forms of cessationist theology seems to be shaped by this rationalism. Third, the missionary to the unreached world must be prepared for real spiritual warfare.

Spiritual Issues and Physical Attacks

While Don's issue was psychological, is it possible for believers to be physically attacked as well in spiritual warfare? In my opinion, the answer is yes, but it seems to most often be a result of unrepentant sin. Only recently, I have observed an individual physically manifest direct bleeding scratches on their body during an all-night prayer meeting. We discerned that the cause was a lack of forgiveness which gave Satan an open door to oppress the person physically. The solution to the problem was not deliverance—exorcising demons from the individual. Instead, it was to help this person repent and forgive those who had harmed them. This situation reminds of the role of extraordinary prayer to reveal the heart of the issue.

Conclusion

The spiritual world is real, and spiritual warfare is real. We need to have a biblical approach regarding spiritual warfare that is focused on God's promises and his provision for us to defeat the enemy. We must also rely on the power of the Holy Spirit. If we are going to bring the gospel to every tribe, tongue, people, and nation, then we must recognize this fact. Westerners will need to move beyond a hyper-rationalistic worldview.

We must also recognize the place of extraordinary prayer in the process. Those of us from the West will need to learn from the Global South missionaries who have so much to teach us about this subject. Though this process will be humbling, it will also open the door to a great harvest amongst the unreached.

Bibliography

Jeremiah, David. *Answers to Questions about Spiritual Warfare*. San Diego: Turning Point, 2020.

Books for Further Study

Bardsley, John. *He Gives Us Authority*. Coventry, UK: WEC Publications, 2012.

Moore, Russell. *Tempted and Tried: Temptation and the Triumph of Christ*. Wheaton, IL: Crossway, 2011.

Murphy, Ed. *The Handbook for Spiritual Warfare: Revised and Updated*. Nashville: Thomas Nelson, 2003.

Rhone, Thomas. *God Still Speaks Through Visions and Dreams*. Raleigh, NC: Pendium, 2016.

Ritchie, Mark Andrew. *Spirit of the Rainforest*. Chicago: Island Lake Press, 2000.

Part Two

Mission in Word—Evangelism

When we praise God, we exalt the one who "is the same yesterday and today and forever" (Heb 13:8 ESV). When we preach the gospel, we proclaim it as "the power of God for salvation to *everyone* who believes" (Rom 1:16 ESV, emphasis added) regardless of where they are coming from. As we will explain in the following chapter, it is the same gospel that we preach, regardless of context, encapsulated by verses from God's word such as John 3:16.

While the word we preach stays the same, the starting places of those with whom we engage in gospel conversations vary greatly, as chapters five through eight make plain. We can, like Paul, confidently "become all things to all people, that by all means [we] might save some … all for the sake of the gospel" (1 Cor 9:22–23 ESV). In this section, we consider how to begin where people are (secular Europeans, Muslims, and those attending public universities around the world, among others) and point them to the God who speaks all languages and is present in all cultures, the God who can give hope in all contexts and circumstances, the God who will be worshiped by all nations, tribes, and tongues, diverse yet united by the Word made flesh.

Chapter 4

Evangelism in One Verse

Bill Jones

Do you ever get confused between the means and the end? I do, especially during my private devotions. Every day, for over fifteen years, I have had what many people call a quiet time, time alone with God, or time for personal devotion. Every day. Granted, many of my times with God were extremely brief. But I checked the box. I went through my routine. I had my devotional time.

I am not claiming my perfect record as a badge of honor, just the opposite. It is to my shame that I have gone over fifteen years without missing a day in personal devotions. Why? Because during far too many of those times alone with God, I never met with God. I focused so much on the means (my routine for God) that I forgot about the end (my relationship with God). Talk about a disconnect.

Fortunately, I am not alone when it comes to focusing so much on the means that the end is forgotten. A lot of people tend to focus so much on the means that they forget the end. Interestingly, there's a corollary to this proposition: sometimes we focus so much on the end that we forget the means.

Unfortunately, that fact just might describe most of us involved in the great cause of missions. We focus so much on completing the task of world evangelization that we forget to focus on the necessary means to accomplish the task. Just in case you missed it, the necessary means.

The church has all kinds of ministries taking place around the world to help penetrate the remaining 42 percent of the world's population who hasn't heard of our Lord Jesus Christ. We are digging wells, distributing food, passing out clothing, providing medical care, translating Scripture, and discipling nationals. All of these are very important and strategic ministries but often these activities occur without evangelism.

Without evangelism, we have no world evangelization. Without evangelism we cannot fulfill the Great Commission. Without evangelism we cannot make Christ's glory known among the nations. Without evangelism we fail to reach the remaining seven thousand unreached people groups.

Notice how these verses connect evangelism and world evangelization. Mark writes, "And He said to them, 'Go into all the world and *preach* the gospel to all creation'" (Mark 16:15 NASB, emphasis added). Luke adds, "And that repentance for forgiveness of sins would be *proclaimed* in His name to all the nations, beginning from Jerusalem" (Luke 24:47 NASB, emphasis added). Luke also writes, "But you will receive power when the Holy Spirit has come upon you and you shall be my *witnesses* both in Jerusalem, and in all Judea and Samaria, and as far as the remotest part of the earth" (Acts 1:8 NASB, emphasis added). In Colossians 1:28–29, one of my life verses, the Apostle Paul writes, "We proclaim him, admonishing every person and teaching every person with all wisdom, so that we may present every person complete in Christ. For this purpose I also labor, striving according to his power, which works mightily within me."

My point is that evangelism is absolutely necessary if we are going to complete the task of world evangelization. Yet, we as the church often fail miserably at evangelism. Sometimes we seem to be able to do everything but share our faith. It is one of the dirty little secrets of the mission field.

Though I don't consider myself an expert at evangelism and often feel like a failure sharing my faith, I love seeing people transformed by the Holy Spirit when they place their faith in Jesus Christ after hearing the message of his love and forgiveness. I love evangelism. As I write I keep thinking about three thirty-somethings with whom I had the privilege of sharing the gospel over the last three weeks. Two days after Will prayed to receive Christ, he joined the Bible study that I teach in our city for businessmen. It is a blessing to watch up him grow. Bert and his wife Suzanne were so enthusiastic to give their lives to Christ after my wife and I shared the gospel with them that they didn't wait to go outside the restaurant and accept Christ in our car. They wanted to pray right then and there at the table with strangers sitting all around us. What a privilege that God would give me and my wife this amazing opportunity.

My journey of learning to share my faith began while I was in college. My mother was in a hospital located near my campus. She called and asked if I would come to see her. When I arrived she asked me whether she would go to heaven or hell if she died during her surgery. Since our family did not go to church, this was a very reasonable question. I responded that I had no clue. How could I? Like my mother, I wasn't a believer. I added, however, that back at my dorm I had a drawer full of some yellow booklets that my friends kept giving me. Supposedly, they explained how a person could cross over into a personal relationship with God. I went back to my dorm, grabbed a "Four Spiritual Laws" booklet from my inventory, and returned to the hospital. As I read this clear explanation of the gospel to my mother, God touched her. When I got to the end and started reading the prayer for salvation, she began repeating the prayer aloud. I was a bit unnerved, but I kept reading, all the way to the "Amen." When I looked up, my mother was visibly changed. I had led my own mother to Christ when I wasn't even a Christian.

Looking back, I realized that it is not the messenger, but the message of the gospel that's most important. In Romans 1:16, the Apostle Paul put it this way: "I am not ashamed of the gospel, for it is the power of God for salvation." Just a few weeks later I gave my own life to Christ.

Over the years God has continued teaching me lessons to become more effective in evangelism, initially as a student minister and then as a church planter. For the last three and a half decades, evangelism has been central to my work serving two organizations—Crossover Global, a church planting organization that I co-founded, and Columbia International University, where I have served as an evangelism professor, president, and now chancellor. By God's grace, Crossover Global has planted over three thousand churches among Muslims and Hindus. Columbia International University educates students from a biblical worldview to impact the nations with the message of Christ. Our graduates are found all over the world serving Christ.

One of the primary lessons I have learned over the years is that we need to keep the message of the gospel simple. Not simplistic, but simple. If we make the gospel simplistic, we leave out vital truths that a seeker needs to understand to cross over into a personal relationship with Christ. Making the message of Christ simple means that we don't add so much content that the unbeliever becomes confused and cannot properly respond. When believers consistently communicate the gospel in simple terms, the evangelistic process becomes reproducible. New Christians can immediately multiply themselves by sharing with others what they have personally received.

The focus of this chapter is on the sowing process of evangelism, not on the cultivating part. Due to the worldview of some people and people groups, it may require months or even years of communication and clarification before they can understand the truths of the gospel. But as soon as they can understand the gospel, we need to be willing and able to clearly communicate the message of forgiveness in Christ.

What follows is a presentation of how I personally share the message of salvation with others. It is the result of years of trying to make the gospel simple so I can effectively share it with unbelievers as well as train believers to lead their families and friends to Christ. Though it's by no means perfect, it has been a help to many who are committed to evangelism, the necessary means of the end goal of world evangelization.

This method is designed to help you with both what to say and what to do in guiding another person through the message of John 3:16. At each step, clearly identified sections (titled *Transition* and *Explanation*) give you an example of what to say in transitioning to and explaining each aspect of believing in Jesus. Feel free to personalize these transitions and explanations. Do not try to memorize the exact wording. Each step also includes a section (called *Action*) which describes what to write or draw on a piece of paper as you give the corresponding explanation.

Introducing the Verse

Transition: Do you feel like you have a personal relationship with God, or do you feel like you're still in the process? May I explain to you what the Bible says about entering into a personal relationship with God?

Action: Take a piece of paper (or a napkin) and write the words of John 3:16 at the very top of the sheet in this particular order. To help you remember this order, note that the middle two phrases both start with the word "that" and both end with a reference to Jesus Christ. Number these phrases in the following order: 1, 3, 4, 2.

John 3:16
1) For God so loved the world
3) that He gave His only begotten Son
4) that whoever believes in Him
2) should not perish but have eternal life.

Explanation: Many people have heard of this verse. The reason John 3:16 is so famous is because it summarizes the core message of the Bible in four spiritual truths.

God's Purpose

Transition: Let's look at the first truth. What does God desire from man?

Action: Put quotation marks around the words "God," "loved," and "world." About halfway down the page, begin to diagram this truth by writing the word "God" on the right, the word "world" on the left, and the word "love" down the middle.

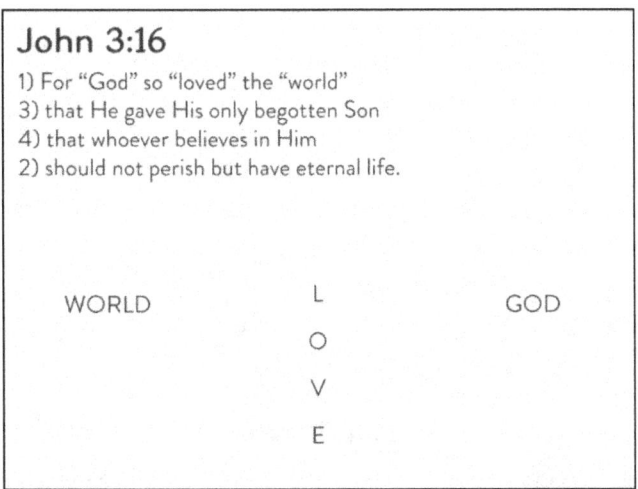

Explanation: God created people to have a personal relationship with him. He wants this relationship to be one of love—one where God shows his love to people and where people show their love to him.

Man's Problem

Transition: Let's look at the second spiritual truth. Why do you think more people are not experiencing this loving personal relationship?

Action: Write the word "sin" below the word "love." Then draw two cliffs, one under the word "world," and one under the word "God."

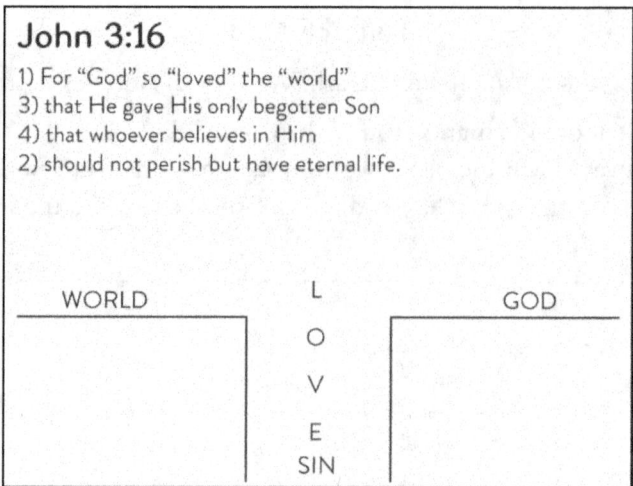

Explanation: It is because of sin. Sin is disobeying God. When someone is offended it causes problems in the relationship. A person's sin, whether in action or attitude, causes a separation between Holy God and man. The Bible calls this separation spiritual death.

Separation

Transition: It's bad enough to be separated from God because of our sin, but it gets worse.

Action: Put quotation marks around the word "perish" and write it under the left-hand cliff (the one with the word "world" on it). Draw an arrow downward from the word "perish" and write the word "hell."

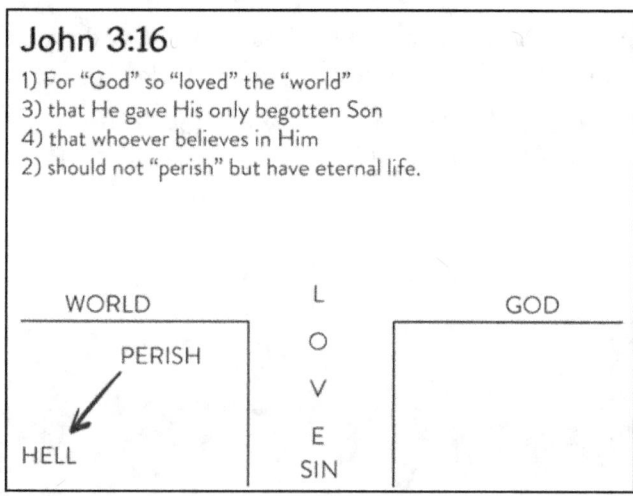

Explanation: The Bible says that if anyone dies physically while separated from God spiritually, he or she will spend eternity in a place called hell.

Hope

Transition: That's bad news, but this second spiritual truth also gives hope.

Action: Put quotation marks around the words "eternal life" and write them under the right-hand cliff. Draw an arrow downward from the words "eternal life" and write the word "heaven."

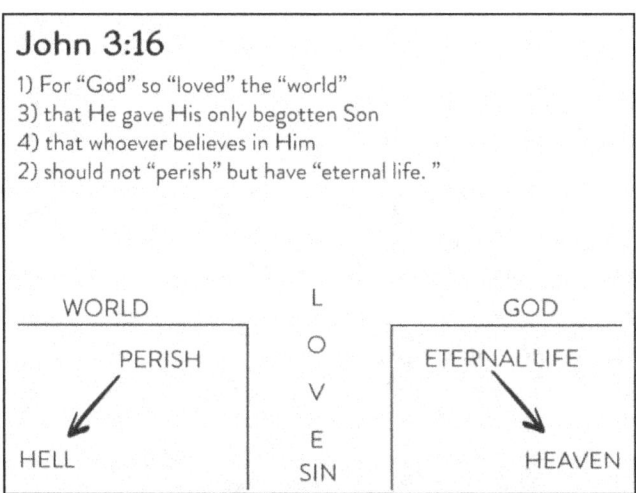

Explanation: God does not want man to spend eternity in hell because of his sin. God desires to have a personal relationship with man so that they can live together forever in a place called heaven.

God's Remedy

Transition: The question then becomes how does one deal with this problem of sin? That leads us to the third spiritual truth.

Action: Put quotation marks around the word "Son" and write it on the diagram so that it shares the "o" of the word "love." Then draw a cross that encloses the words "Son" and "love" and bridges the two cliffs.

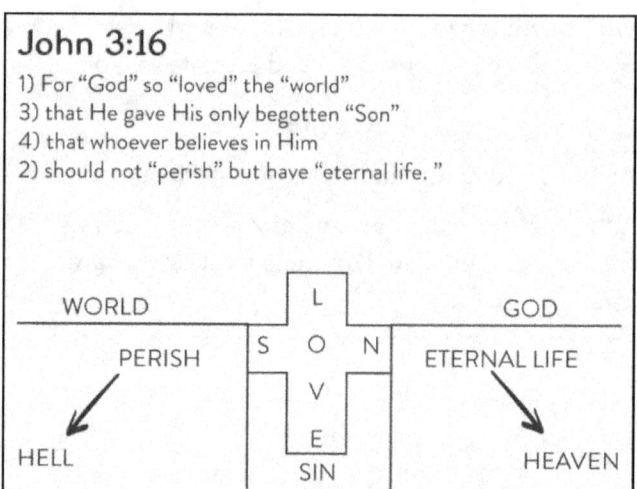

Explanation: God took care of the sin problem by sending his Son, Jesus Christ, to eliminate the separation between us and God. After living a perfect life for thirty-three years, Christ was willingly crucified on a cross to pay the penalty for our sins. After he was buried, to the shock of those who loved him and those who hated him, he rose from the dead. His resurrection accomplished two things: it paid for sin and established a bridge between God and us.

Man's Response

Transition: The question now is how can a person cross over the bridge that Christ has provided and personally experience God's love and forgiveness? The fourth spiritual truth gives the answer.

Action: Draw an arching arrow from the word "world" to the word "God." Put quotation marks around the words "believes in Him" and write them on the arrow as shown.

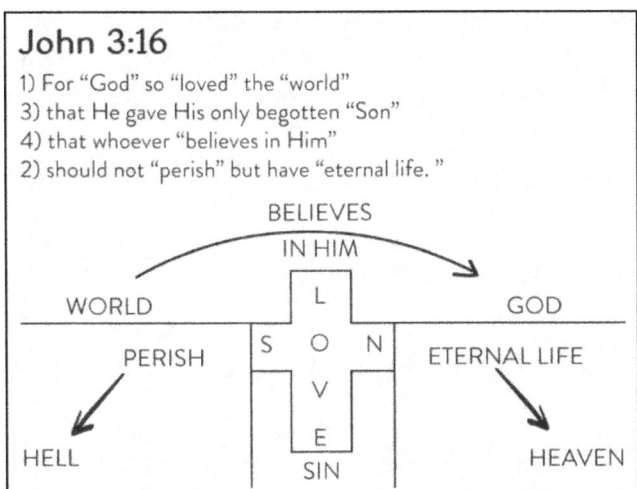

Explanation: Most people think a person crosses over by being good. Yet, one could never be good enough to get to a holy God. Crossing over into a right relationship with God comes by trusting Christ to take you across, rather than by trying to get across through your own efforts. A right relationship with God is received from Christ by faith, not achieved for Christ by works.

Inviting a Decision

Transition: May we personalize this for a moment?

Action: Underline the word "whoever."

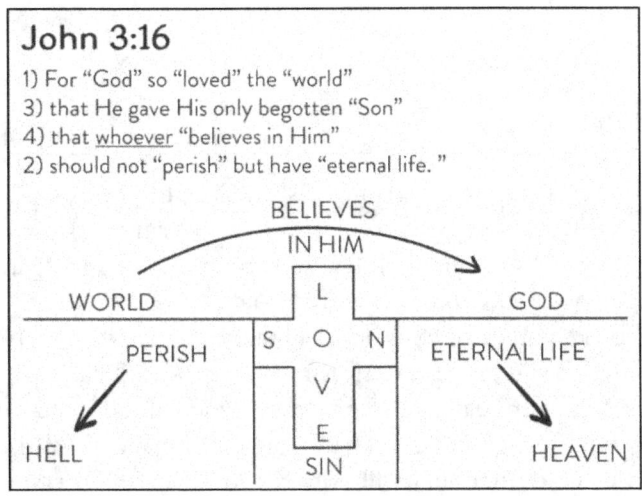

Explanation: Where would you put yourself on this diagram? (Note: If they put themselves on the right-hand side, ask them to tell you when they crossed over. If they put themselves on the left-hand side, or on top of the cross, ask the next question.)

Do you see anything keeping you from trusting Christ to take you across to God right now? (Note: If they say "yes," ask them what their questions are and deal with them accordingly. If you do not know the answer to a question, tell them you will try to find out and get back to them with the answer. If they say "no," prepare to lead them in prayer expressing their desire to God.)

Guiding in Prayer

Transition: If you desire to trust Christ to make you right with God, you can do so right now.

Action: In the diagram, place the number 1 next to the word "God," the number 2 next to the word "world," the number 3 next to the cross, and the number 4 beside the word "believes."

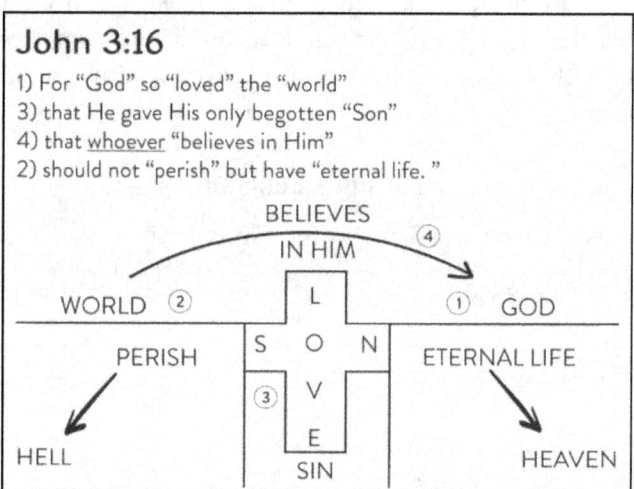

Explanation: You can express your trust in Christ by telling God: (1) that you are thankful that he loves you; (2) that you are sorry for your sin which has separated you from him; (3) that you are grateful that he gave his only Son to forgive your sin and give you eternal life; and (4) that you believe Christ will make you right with him, right now.

I can pray and you can repeat after me. Remember, what is most important is the attitude of your heart, not the words of your mouth. You can pray the right words, but if your heart is not truly convinced that only Christ can make you right with God, then you will not cross over to God. Let's pray. (Note: Pray the above four truths to God, pausing so the seeker can pray after you.)

Chapter 5

Evangelism in a Secular World

Raphael Anzenberger

Introduction

Could we imagine a world where the leader of an LGBTQ movement provides the blueprints for an innovative church plant? Where a radical-left politician is captured by the beauty of Jesus? Where fashion designers enjoy talking theology with evangelical professors? I live in such a world—a world where the gospel still works as the power of salvation for those who seek after God. The secular world is a wonderful playground for the church. It provides breathtaking opportunities to share the hope we have within us. But it also requires a very different posture than that of "an evangelical church under attack." What are the best practices to engage the secular mind? And why should we engage the secular world at all?

Understanding the Times

To better engage the secular world with the gospel, we first need to get a clear understanding of the landscape. *Secularization* is a historical process with both positive and negative aspects. Lesslie Newbigin writes: "Negatively, it is the withdrawal of areas of life and activity from the control of organized religious bodies, and the withdrawal of areas of thought from the control of what are believed to be revealed religious truths."[1] This withdrawal has been the source of much tension for the church. The historical process started in the pre-Reformation age and continues today at various speeds and in different places.

The result of the secularization process is *secularity*, a snapshot of the secularization process at a specific time. In *A Secular Age*, Charles Taylor defines secularity in three modes:

(1) That which is retreating in the public space (plurality of beliefs);

(2) A type of belief and practice which is or is not a regression (decline of religious beliefs);

---
1 Newbigin, *Honest Religion*, 8.

(3) A certain kind of belief or commitment whose conditions in this age are being examined (conditions of religious belief).[2]

The secularization process will lead to different stages of modes of secularity depending on where one lives. It is typically at its peak in academic circles and at its lowest in rural areas. The secular world will look different at Harvard than in rural Kentucky.

Secularization is a process, while *secularism* is a system of belief. The two cannot be used synonymously. Newbigin adds:

> I take "secularism" to refer to a system of belief, or an attitude, which in principle denies the existence or the significance of realities other than those which can be measured by the methods of natural science … It was defined at the Jerusalem meeting of the International Missionary Council (1928) as "a way of life and an interpretation of life that include only the natural order of things and that do not find God, or a realm of spiritual reality, necessary for life or thought."[3]

Secularism claims that God is not necessary for one to be happy. It is different from atheism since atheism denies the existence of God. Secularism is closer to a self-sufficient humanism.

We must acknowledge widespread secularism in the West. It is a definite marker of our contemporary societies. Taylor defines our times as the *secular age*, "one in which the eclipse of all goals beyond human flourishing becomes conceivable; or better, it falls within the range of an imaginable life for masses of people."[4]

It's difficult for an evangelical Christian to imagine that one could be happy without God. In reality, however, secularism is the norm, and unbelief is the default mode of belief. In a secular world, the evangelical believer is the exception—the exception to the current narrative of self-fulfillment. I learned this the hard way when I attended my first parent picnic at my son's French kindergarten. "What do you do for living?" asked one guest. I responded, "I am a pastor." He then called his friends around and said, "Look, I have found a guy who believes that there is a God. Extraordinary! I thought you guys only existed in a museum!" Later that year, I handed him the manuscript of my first book entitled, *I Wish I Could Believe But*. Let's just say he was not very happy with me. He asked, "Are you saying that I cannot be fulfilled if God is not in my life?" For this man (happily

---

2 Taylor, *Secular Age*, 4.

3 Newbigin, *Honest Religion*, 8.

4 Taylor, *Secular Age*, 19–20.

married, with two beautiful children, usually windsurfing in Morocco during holidays), the prospect of a better life looked implausible. I replied, "This is exactly what I meant to write." I had encountered secularism at its peak. He was the norm and I was the exception.

If we truly understand our predicament, the only way forward is to engage secularism instead of retreating from it. Newbigin asserts:

> There are at least three ways in which the opposition between religion and the secular is referred to in current Christian writing. Firstly, a secular *society* is described as one in which the citizen is not subject to pressure from the state, or from the organs of society, to conform to a particular set of beliefs. Secondly, a secular *ethic* is described as one which does not subordinate the actual concrete decision to an alleged supra-natural law or standard but permits it to be made on the basis of the empirical realities of the situation in each case. Thirdly, a secular *style* of life for the Christian is described as one which does not turn away from the world to seek God but finds God by involvement in the life of the world. I hope that the discussion of these three issues will help us make more precise distinctions, and to indicate the sense in which a Christian must still be a religious man and a secular man at the same time.[5]

The withdrawal of Christianity from the public square, combined with the challenge of a secular ethic, is the source of much anxiety in evangelicalism, giving space and credibility for emerging populist movements. Bruce Ashford adds:

> Over the course of the past half-century, many American evangelicals have put their eggs in the basket of short-term political activism—with the emphasis on the political and the short-term ... we reduced culture to politics, and politics to short-term activism, assuming a large part of the remedy to our social and cultural ills lies in a quick political fix. Repeatedly, we've treated each presidential election or midterm election as the one that—despite all historical evidence to the contrary—will finally deliver our hopes and ease our fears.[6]

Secularization, secularity, secularism, and a secular age are profound sociological concepts that frame evangelism in the secular world. So how do we share the gospel in such an age?

---

5 Newbigin, *Honest Religion*, 123.
6 Ashford, "Politics and Public Life," 96.

Redeeming the Times

Most recent apologetics sources address secularism from the perspective of worldviews, comparing the Christian faith with the different *-isms* of secularism (e.g., hedonism, materialism, rationalism). I have not found this approach very helpful. Most secular people don't know what they believe, let alone why. I have found Taylor's approach much more effective. He writes:

> In order to get a little bit clearer on this level, I want to talk about belief and unbelief, not as rival theories, that is, ways that people account for existence, or morality, whether by God or by something in nature, or whatever. Rather what I want to do is focus attention on the different kinds of lived experience involved in understanding your life in one way or the other, on what it's like to live as a believer or an unbeliever.[7]

Describing the lived experience of the secular person, Taylor continues:

> There is a kind of stabilized middle condition, to which we often aspire. This is one where we have found a way to escape the forms of negation, exile, and emptiness, without having reached fullness. We come to terms with the middle position, often through some stable, even routine order in life, in which we are doing things which have some meaning for us; for instance, which contribute to our ordinary happiness, or which are fulfilling in various ways, or which contribute to what we conceive of as the good. Or often, in the best scenario, all three: for instance, we strive to live happily with spouse and children, while practicing a vocation which we find fulfilling, and also which constitutes an obvious contribution to human welfare.[8]

Think back to the conversation at the kindergarten picnic table. This man was living a happy life with his spouse and children, even enjoying surfing in Morocco. Reading my manuscript created a certain level of destabilization of this middle condition, but not enough to make him question his belief. Routines are strongholds that keep the secular mind locked in its own narrative of happiness and fulfillment.

This was also true of the prodigal son (Luke 15:11–32 ESV). Trapped at home in the routine of boredom (sick of home), he takes off in hopes of finding a better life. The journey starts in his own heart where he convinces himself that his father owes him something (relativism). He sets out alone (individualism) and lives a "joyful life" (hedonism), spending his

---

7 Taylor, *Secular Age*, 4.

8 Taylor, 6.

father's money (materialism). Then he hits rock bottom. He experiences a profound disruption to his newly formed routine—no more money, no more pleasure, not even pigs' food, just absurdity (cynicism).

Luke tells us that "when he came to himself" (Luke 15:17 ESV) and repented, the prodigal son realized that he was actually homesick. This realization sends him on his journey back home. He had been home, was sick of home, became homesick, and then returned home. This is the four-part story for all human beings. The prodigal son was living in the middle, caught between being sick of home and homesick. All the *-isms* in the story are symptoms of this middle condition, a lived experience more than a grand theory of life.

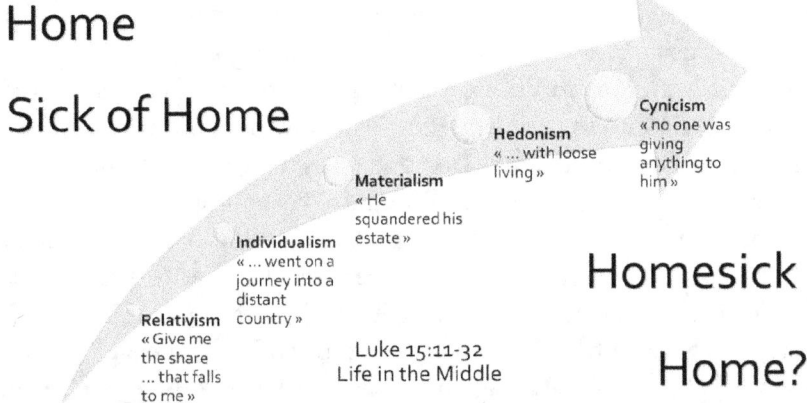

Luke 15:11-32
Life in the Middle

Most people in our church who came to faith started their journey because of a profound disruption in their routine (e.g., COVID-19, divorce, job loss, or sickness). This disruption causes the secular narrative of happiness to crumble. Since there is no theology of suffering in secularism, no philosophical categories can make sense of their inner contradiction and doubt. They are only left to question. On the other hand, the journey of faith begins with repentance and turning away from our own stories to seek a greater story—a story that will lead us home. Newbigin said it well:

> Skepticism is not the active principle in the advance of knowledge. The active principle is the willingness to go out beyond what is certain, to listen to what is not yet clear, to search for what is hardly visible, to venture the affirmation which may prove to be wrong, but which may also prove to be the starting point for new conquests of the mind. In the traditional language of Christianity the name for that active principle is faith.[9]

---

9 Newbigin, *Honest Religion*, 84.

So, as we seek to understand and redeem the times, we must pay attention to the disruptors in the lives of our friends and colleagues whose lives continue to collapse in a fragile world.

Seizing the Times

In 2008, InterVarsity Christian Fellowship released a study tracing the faith journeys of their students. Their findings resembled what I observed happening in Europe. When students came to faith in Christ, they crossed five distinct thresholds: trust, curiosity, openness, seeking, and following.

The first threshold, trust, is what I call the sociological threshold. When approaching someone with the gospel, the default mode we encounter is distrust. They are asking, "Who are you and what do you want from me?" I am now living in Montreal, and I find the same distrust mode in Canadians. They ask accusingly, "How can you identify yourself as a Christian when so much harm was done to the First Nations (indigenous peoples)?" We are guilty by association. The challenge is to help move our non-believing friends from a place of distrust to trust. Doing so takes time, courage, and patience.

I call the second threshold, curiosity, the philosophical threshold. Though a non-believer might trust a Christian, they may still remain apathetic to the Christian faith. The French philosopher, Jean-Paul Sartre, famously said, "If God existed, that would make no difference."[10] Again, it requires time and energy to engage with philosophical questions and to challenge the secular narrative. But the curiosity stage truly begins when we share our personal testimonies and live out the gospel in words and deeds.

I refer to the third threshold, openness, as the existential threshold. A person might trust you, be curious, and even ask questions, but that does not mean they want to change. Openness to change requires repentance—"coming to one's self." It is the most complicated and challenging threshold I have found, so much patience is required.

The fourth threshold, seeking, is what I call the worldview threshold. Here seekers might explore the various options offered in a pluralistic society (e.g., environmentalism, Eastern mysticism), which all tell different stories for how to find fulfillment. At this stage, the goal is not to get lost in a full-scale exploration of worldviews, but rather to help the person encounter Jesus. At this stage, I have found investigative Bible studies to be very effective.

---

10 Sartre, "Existentialism Is a Humanism."

I call the last stage, following, the spiritual threshold because coming to faith in Christ is a spiritual matter. While we present the person and work of Christ, the Holy Spirit is the one doing the work of regeneration. It is pure joy when someone encounters the Lord in saving faith and a great disappointment when others reject him and continue their search.

Conclusion

Is it possible to engage the secular West with the gospel? Yes. The secular landscape offers unprecedented opportunities for gospel engagement when approaching secularism with the right posture. I am reminded of the words of Newbigin: "It is difficult to read the whole story of the human quest for knowledge without coming to the conclusion that it is more dangerous to be afraid of making a mistake than to be afraid of missing something real."[11] Let us not be afraid to engage the secular mind. If we do not speak, they will be missing something real—eternal life. Our task is to understand, redeem time, and seize the times. The rest of the work belongs to Christ and Christ alone.

Bibliography

Ashford, Bruce Riley. "Politics and Public Life in a Secular Age." In *Our Secular Age: Ten Years of Reading and Applying Charles Taylor*. Edited by Collin Hansen, 87–98. Deerfield, IL: Gospel Coalition, 2017.

Newbigin, Lesslie. *The Gospel in a Pluralist Society*. Grand Rapids: Eerdmans, 1989.

Newbigin, Lesslie. *Honest Religion for Secular Man*. London: SCM Press, 1996.

Sartre, Jean-Paul. "Existentialism Is a Humanism." Accessed February 14, 2023. https://www.marxists.org/reference/archive/sartre/works/exist/sartre.htm.

Taylor, Charles. *A Secular Age*. Cambridge, MA: Harvard University Press, 2007.

---

11 Newbigin, *Honest Religion*, 84.

Chapter 6
Gospel-Centered Relationships with Muslims

Trevor Castor

The historic relationship between Muslims and Christians has ebbed and flowed between times of peaceful coexistence, avoidance, and bloodshed. Even during times of peace, mutual misunderstandings pervade, and the relationship is tenuous at best. Eventually, mutuality disintegrates into an "us versus them" framework and each group's identity is solidified by viewing the other as a common enemy. Considering that a little more than half of the world's population self-ascribes to one of these two faith communities, it seems imperative for Christians to take a different approach—one defined by the fruits of the Spirit rather than the ever-tempting clash of civilizations paradigm.

A different approach does not mean that we must agree to disagree and keep our distance from one another. Nor does it mean pretending that we believe the same things or seeking the lowest common denominator. As we develop deeper relationships with Muslims, differences will indeed arise. When they do, we should strive to have these conversations with a posture of humility and love rather than arrogance. Whether or not Muslims decide to take such an approach does not absolve Christians from doing so. We must heed the call to fearlessly proclaim the kingdom of God with wisdom and gentleness. Below are a few principles that will help Christians develop meaningful relationships with Muslims and hopefully avoid being unnecessarily offensive. Most importantly, these principles will help to ensure that the gospel remains central in our relationship with Muslims so that they can encounter our risen Lord.

Avoid Comparisons

There is no need to make Islam look bad in order for Christianity to look good. When Christians and Muslims talk about their faith with each other, comparisons are inevitable, but that does not mean they should be a strategy. We will hear each other's beliefs and naturally consider points of similarity and difference. This response is to be expected. Understanding of something new often comes through comparing it with what we already know. We might be tempted to accelerate this process by making comparisons for Muslims, but doing so is unhelpful. This style of evangelism is popular with media ministries, and there is more than enough content online, so we do not need to take such an approach. When we talk with Muslims, we want to make sure our focus is on sharing what we believe rather than disproving Islam. We do not want our love for Jesus to be overshadowed by our opinions about Islam.

Muhammad and Jesus

There is no need to make Muhammad look bad for Jesus to look good. When Christians discuss Jesus with Muslims, a temptation may arise to begin making comparisons between Jesus and Muhammad. This can quickly escalate into what is reminiscent of two schoolchildren arguing about whose dad would win in a fight. The Christian's goal in such an approach is to try and show Christ's superiority over Muslims' beloved prophet. However, showing Christ's supremacy over all created things can be done without diminishing that which is adored by Muslims. Comparing "the Son [who] is the radiance of God's glory and the exact representation of his being" (Heb 1:3 NIV) with any created thing is not a worthwhile endeavor and may even diminish Christ in the mind of the hearer because of the negative views of Muhammad articulated in the process. Imagine someone trying to tell you how lovely their spouse is by insulting your spouse. Not only would you find the person offensive, but you might also conclude that their spouse is not as great as they imagine. Maybe the well-known parental advice is appropriate here, "If you don't have anything nice to say, then don't say anything at all." Or, better yet, "Do to others as you would have them do to you" (Luke 6:31 NIV). Muslims will go to great lengths to defend the reputation of Muhammad. Some have even acted out in violence against those who insult their prophet. We do not need to express an opinion about Muhammad in order to share Christ with Muslims. If you do have negative opinions about Muhammad, it may be best to keep them to yourself lest they become the stumbling block for Muslims meeting Christ.

Avoiding comparisons between Jesus and Muhammad does not mean avoiding the topic of Jesus. We must not hedge on our Christian faith to love Muslims. On the contrary, we should talk to our Muslim friends about Christ early and often. Keep in mind that Jesus holds a prominent position in Islam as a prophet. Of course, Christian ideas about his death, resurrection, and divinity will be an obstacle and may even be offensive to Muslims. This fact is understandable since Paul tells us that Christ crucified can be both a stumbling block and foolishness to those who do not believe. I can understand why Muslims refuse to believe that God would allow Jesus to die because it can seem unjust. I can also understand why Muslims struggle with the concept of Christ's divinity. After all, it took Peter two years of walking with Jesus before confessing that he was the Messiah. Even after this was revealed, Peter initially refused to believe that Christ's death was a necessary part of our redemption (Matt 16:21–22 NIV). Only after the apostles encountered the risen Lord were their wrong assumptions about Jesus and the kingdom brought to light. They were looking for a Davidic king and kingdom. Instead, they got death on a cross, a crown of thorns, and a sign that mocked Jesus as "King of the Jews." Only after the resurrection could they see that Christ's life was not taken from him but laid down by him as a ransom for many.

Do not assume that Muslims will comprehend the nature of Christ or his work on the cross any quicker than the disciples did. Be willing to share about Jesus as much as your Muslim friend is willing to listen. When you do talk about Jesus, consider sharing stories where the hearers are left with the question, *Who is this man*? Think of all the times people asked that question in the New Testament. Who is this man that calms the sea, forgives sin, raises the dead, and heals so many? Muslims agree with us that Jesus was indeed a man, but maybe these stories will help to reveal that there is more to him than his humanity.

The Bible and the Qur'an

Another tempting comparison is the Bible versus the Qur'an. There is nothing wrong with looking at two religious texts side by side so long as you do it charitably. However, what often happens is that violent verses from the Qur'an are taken out of context and compared with the pacifistic teachings of Jesus. A better approach would be to recognize that both the Bible and the Qur'an have difficult passages encouraging violence as well as other behaviors that are unacceptable in the twenty-first century. Christians will often brush away difficult passages in the Bible by claiming that they are irrelevant because they are in the Old Testament. This is reminiscent of Marcion's (ca. AD 85–ca. AD 160) heresy that the vengeful god of the Old Testament was different than the loving god of the New Testament.

The point is, both Christians and Muslims have worked painstakingly on various systems for interpreting their texts. If you are not using the Muslim exegetical tradition, do not quote the Qur'an in hopes of proving a point. We dislike it when unbelievers misuse the Bible to make a mockery of Christianity, so why do it to Muslims?

Not comparing the Bible with the Qur'an does not mean avoiding the Bible. You might be surprised that many Muslims want to read the Bible. I will never forget the time that I brought a student named Luke with me to meet a Muslim family that needed help with English tutoring. When we got into my car, he asked me if it was okay for him to wear his cross necklace. I asked him if he put it on just for the Muslim family or if he always wore it. He replied, "I always wear it." I told him to keep it on. The next question took me off guard. He asked, "Is it okay if I bring my Bible inside with me to meet the family?" I asked whether he typically brought his Bible with him when meeting someone for the first time and he replied "yes." So, I told him to bring it with him and to not feel the need to change what he would do naturally just because we were meeting a Muslim family. I wanted him to feel comfortable being himself.

After going through introductions, we sat down for tea and cookies. The father of the family asked about Luke's book. I told him it was a Bible. The father then asked Luke to read something aloud. Luke proceeded to read a short passage from the Psalms. When the father heard it, tears filled his eyes and he proceeded to ask me if I also owned a Bible. I told him that I did. I will never forget what came next. He said, "It's like you have had a light this whole time and you have been hiding it from us." He basically told me I had been hiding a lamp under a basket. I was so embarrassed that I wanted to run out of the room! I apologized and told him from then on, every time I came to his house, I would have a Bible story ready. That day changed my life. Ever since then, when I meet a Muslim, I try and share something from the Scriptures. Since I am not accustomed to carrying my Bible with me everywhere like Luke, I share something that I have memorized, and it is always received with gratitude. I have come to realize that this is what most Muslims expect from a person who says they love God.

Religious Histories

Comparing religious histories is also a bad idea. Again, it is not necessarily wrong to look at two religious histories side by side if it is done carefully and with integrity. However, much like the textual comparison, this approach tends to compare the best representations of Christians with the worst representations of Muslims. This is dishonest and not Christlike. Muslims and Christians both have troubling past and present expressions of their faiths. Both are guilty of religious violence against each other and against their own faith communities. I am reminded of a conversation with Christian History professor Mike Barnett after President Obama tweeted "ISIL is not 'Islamic.' No religion condones the killing of innocents, and the vast majority of ISIL's victims have been Muslim."[1] Dr. Barnett commented that it would have been more accurate to say that every religion, at some point, condoned the killing of innocents, including their own people.[2]

I was painfully reminded of Christian intra-religious violence while touring an Anglican church next to the Martyrs Memorial in Oxford, England. While admiring the courage of the Protestant reformers, a local guide asked me if I had visited the memorial to the Catholic martyrs. Only a few blocks away, I found a small plaque memorializing two Catholic priests and two laymen who were hanged by Protestants for their Catholic faith. The priests' body parts were displayed throughout the city of Oxford as a warning that practicing Catholicism was punishable as an act of treason. In fewer than forty years, both Catholics and Protestants were martyred in Oxford by one another for their different expressions of Christianity. Some may argue that these deaths had less to do with religious belief and more to do with political power. However, the same arguments are made by many Muslims in the twenty-first century regarding groups like Al-Qaeda and ISIS. We should allow Muslims to speak for themselves rather than allowing the actions of radicals to define the more than 1.8 billion Muslims spanning the globe. The Oxford memorials demonstrate the reality that religious violence is not exclusively a Muslim problem—it is a human one. This is all the more reason we should approach Muslims from a position of seeing the plank in our own eye before making judgments about the violence of Muslim communities (Matt 7:3–5 NIV). We should also be willing to engage in corporate repentance for the ways in which misguided, zealous Christians have mistreated Muslims rather than trying to distance ourselves from past sins of our heritage.

See Muslims as Image Bearers

All Muslims, including Muhammad, bear the image of God and therefore have inherent value and the potential to reflect God's character and glory

---

[1] Barack Obama, Twitter post, September 11, 2014.

[2] Dr. Barnett was the first Dean of the College of Intercultural Studies at CIU. He went to be with the Lord in 2015.

(Gen 1:26–28 NIV). We should consider this fact as we interact with Muslims. Your speech and actions are an opportunity to demonstrate what a life hidden with Christ looks like. We should avoid the temptation to curse any image-bearer with the same tongue that praises the one whose image they bear (Jas 3:9 NIV). Consider spending more time seeking the image of God in your Muslim friends and less time looking for how the image might be distorted. In other words, be on the lookout for where God is working in the lives of Muslims and give him the credit. The same goes for aspects of Muslim practices that are genuinely biblical. For example, when a Muslim is hospitable, demonstrates care for parents, shows concern for the poor, or is faithful in their prayers, tell them you thank God for giving them these desires. Or you could say something like, "I see that in every way you are very religious" (Acts 17:22 NIV). Ask if you can pray for them and thank God for working in their lives.

Yes, you can pray in the name of Jesus. Muslims know that you think Jesus is God. I have never had a Muslim refuse prayer or take offense that I pray to God the Father in the name of his son Jesus Christ. Remember that your prayers are sacred and that by inviting a Muslim to participate, they will meet God in a new way. You may find that your Muslim friend will begin coming to you with prayer requests. Do not say I will pray for you and send them on their way; rather, pray immediately. Before you leave their home, ask if you can pray a blessing over their household. I cannot overstate the importance of praying with your Muslim friends. If you do not take the opportunity to do so, the assumption may be that you do not pray at all.

Listen to Their Stories

When I did my doctoral research, I would ask my Muslim participants to share their stories with me. Almost without fail, when they finished sharing their story, they would ask me to share mine. Hearing someone's story will give you a deep sense of connection with the person and provide insight into how to pray.

When you get a chance to share your story, do not glorify your sinful life before coming to Christ. "Amazing" testimonies about deliverance from addictions and immorality may not be received the same way by Muslims as they are by Christians. Airing your previous dirty laundry may be considered shameful and offensive rather than a testimony of God's grace. Instead of taking the typical approach of life before and after Christ, think of your story as an opportunity to share how God has been pursuing a relationship with you ever since he formed you in your mother's womb

(Ps 139:13–14; Jer 1:5 NIV). Be sure to emphasize that the peace you have with God and your confidence in approaching his throne is because of the assurance that your sins are forgiven. Speak about being with him one day in heaven and the joy of your salvation here and now. Most Muslims have no assurance of salvation and often are terrified of the Day of Judgment. Your confidence in the grace and mercy of God will be refreshing.

In addition to sharing your life stories, look for opportunities to share life together. Muslims need to see your faith in practice. For Muslims, faith without works is dead. A godly person will demonstrate their love for God through charitable deeds. Yes, we are saved by grace through faith in Christ. We are also set apart in Christ to do good works that he prepares for us (Eph 2:9, 10 NIV). So, live out your faith authentically and in front of your Muslim friends by conforming your life to the image of Christ. Share with them the importance of prayer, fasting, and serving the poor. And when you fail to live perfectly as Christ did, share how you still have peace with God no matter the good you do or fail to do because of the cross.

Conclusion

Confessing Christ as Lord is not simply a process of cognitive assent but of spiritual illumination. Few, if any, Muslims will be argued into the kingdom of God with wisdom, eloquent speech, or by attacking their beliefs with poor comparisons. The reality is that our faith may be considered foolish to Muslims despite our deep convictions (1 Cor 1:17–18 NIV). This is to be expected since our faith is in a King and a kingdom that is not of this world. Loving your enemies, blessing those who persecute you, and taking up a cross in order to truly live is indeed foolish in the eyes of unbelievers. While our faith defies the conventional wisdom of the world, we should still be prepared to testify to the power of the cross as our hope in this world and the one to come (1 Pet 3:15 NIV).

Finally, remember that the Holy Spirit is the one who reveals the true identity of Jesus to a person (2 Cor 4:4 NIV). Consider the possibility that the Holy Spirit is already at work in the lives of Muslims even if they do not believe that the Spirit exists. Without the work of the Holy Spirit, our words will fall on deaf ears and our good deeds will go unnoticed. This reminder is not meant to be discouraging, but reassuring. We should take comfort in knowing that we will never convert a single soul. If Muslims following Jesus were up to us, it would be too heavy a burden for anyone to bear. However, we are called to be a living witness for Christ and the kingdom of God initiated through his death and resurrection. While the Holy Spirit has the job of convicting the world of sin and drawing people into a new life in Christ, our role is to be the one who reveals what that new life looks like and how to pursue it. He has chosen us, his church, to be co-laborers with him in extending an invitation to Muslims to become part of his royal priesthood and chosen possession. So, walk alongside your Muslim friends and pray for the Holy Spirit to demonstrate the love and power of God both in and through you along the way!

Further Reading

Castor, Trevor, and Edward L. Smither. "Timothy I of Baghdad: A Model for Peaceful Dialogue." In *The History of Apologetics: A Biographical and Methodological Introduction*. Edited by Benjamin Forrest et al. 197–209. Grand Rapids, MI: Zondervan, 2020.

Dale, Moyra. *Islam and Women: Hagar's Heritage*. Oxford: Regnum, 2021.

Garrison, David. *A Wind in the House of Islam: How God Is Drawing Muslims around the World to Faith in Jesus Christ*. Monument, CO: WigTake, 2014.

Glaser, Ida, and Hannah Kay. *Thinking Biblically about Islam: Genesis, Transfiguration, Transformation*. Carlisle, UK: Langham, 2016.

Zwemer Center for Muslim Studies. Accessed February 7, 2023. https://www.zwemercenter.com.

Chapter 7

Building God's Kingdom in Public Universities

Danny McCain

Abraham Kuyper is well known for saying: "There is not a square inch in the whole domain of our human existence over which Christ, who is Sovereign over all, does not cry: 'Mine!'" However, what is less well-known is that he made this statement in Amsterdam in 1880 at the opening of a new university.[1] If Christ is going to be Lord of the universe, he must be Lord of the world's universities.

In 1986, while teaching a course on world religions, the first sentence of the textbook's chapter on Judaism caught my attention: "At a time when a good deal of theological discussion is engendered by the Jewish state in the middle east and when *departments of Jewish studies are a part of many universities in Europe and America*, a study like this is a matter of course."[2] I wrote two questions in the margin of my textbook: *Who started them? Who funded them?* Later, I learned that Muslim governments, agencies, and individuals were also sponsoring hundreds of academics and placing them in the world's public universities.

Based on these observations, a group of church leaders met in Overland Park, Kansas in 1986 to explore the possibility of developing a similar model to promote Christian studies in the world's mainstream public universities. This meeting led to the creation of the International Institute for Christian Studies (IICS, now known as Global Scholars).[3] The goal was to penetrate and positively influence public universities globally for Christ.

In 1987, IICS contracted with Rivers State University in Port Harcourt, Nigeria to create an in-service training program for pastors and church leaders. In September 1988, my family and I moved to Nigeria to implement

---

1 Henderson, "Kuyper's Inch," 12–14.
2 Leuner, "Judaism," 49.
3 See the Global Scholars website for more information https://global-scholars.org/.

that program. Later, we relocated to the University of Jos in north-central Nigeria to create a similar program and to work in an existing Department of Religious Studies where I still serve. In 1990, IICS sent three academics to Ukraine, Belarus, and Russia. Since that time, we have placed over 311 academics in 148 universities, spanning fifty-four countries and twenty-two broadly defined academic disciplines.

Originally, we were a typical missionary organization. We recruited missionary academics from the West and sent them to other parts of the world. We did not have a good way to partner with local Christian academics. Around 2010, we began to realize that this failure seriously limited our strategy. After extensive investigation of the needs of the international academic world, we launched the Society of Christian Scholars in February 2020, which identifies, recruits, orients, empowers, and links Christian scholars around the world to do God's kingdom work in public universities. The society provides fourteen services to Christian scholars, including encouragement through digital meetings, a digital library, editing services, in-person conferences, grants, and much more. Over three hundred academics from universities all over the world have joined this society.

My thirty-four years of living and working in two Nigerian public universities and the experiences of my colleagues in other universities have provided valuable lessons about serving God in public universities in Africa and elsewhere.

Teaching in a Public University Is Possible

Many universities in the international community, especially in the developing world, want contact with international institutions and experts. Shortly after I arrived in Jos in 1991, I met a Pakistani scholar who was teaching Islamic studies at the University of Jos. He was seconded to the university from the Saudi Arabian Embassy, which paid his salary. Later I was told he was only one of about seventy expatriate scholars being sponsored by Saudi Arabia to teach in Nigeria.

Over the last three decades, Global Scholars has placed eighteen academics in Nigerian public universities and seven elsewhere in Africa. Combined, these twenty-five Christian scholars have served more than 150 academic years.

Universities in developing countries often have greater flexibility than more established universities. They are open to new collaborations even with Christian organizations. For example, the small West African country of The Gambia is 89 percent Muslim. A visiting team of scholars pointed out to the University of The Gambia some years ago that since they had a department of Islamic studies, they should also have a department of Christian studies. In 2015, Global Scholars helped the university start one. In 2020, the program graduated its first cohort of students. Global Scholars now sponsors two academics who teach in that department.

Historically, Christians have been good at creating ministries in public universities. Organizations like Cru, InterVarsity, and other campus ministries have successfully entered universities from the outside to do evangelism and discipleship. However, Christians can also get jobs as academics and have powerful ministries working from the inside.

Teaching in a Public University Is Strategic

Christian academics in public universities enjoy several key strategic advantages. They have *instant credibility* because nearly everyone respects people with advanced university degrees. They enjoy *theological neutrality* since public universities are not made up of one denomination or theological perspective. They benefit from *academic freedom* because the criteria for success in public universities is excellence, not a theological litmus test, which works out well for evangelicals. Christian academics also experience *reduced visa problems*. When foreign academics work for government institutions, the government assumes immigration responsibility. University teaching also helps with *cost-effective ministry* because there is no need to build buildings or hire support staff. Teachers are also generally placed in a *strategic location*. Academics in public universities serve in the most important institution in the world for social change. Finally, they enjoy a *positive influence*. Good academics can influence the profile and programs of host universities.

Global Scholars has donated thousands of books to university libraries. We have created two academic programs at the University of Jos. We have been able to secure university appointments for former students and staff who share our philosophy. We have mentored many junior scholars who will remain at their universities long after we are gone. We have helped create a campus-wide ministry of Christian academics who meet regularly for prayer and to plan ministry. We have written textbooks that are used in universities, seminaries, Bible colleges, and mission schools. I believe the universities where Global Scholars staff have served are better off today because of the ministry of the Christian academics who have served there.

Christian academics in public universities have a strategic platform. Global Scholars academics are not tentmakers. We do not seek employment in the university so that we can do our "real ministry." Our primary ministry field is the university. However, once a person has a position in a university, many other avenues of ministry often become open.

Serving the Church

Over the last thirty years, I have spoken about fifty times a year at local churches, conferences, and conventions. I have also taught as an adjunct at three seminaries and two mission schools. I have written over thirty books and manuals for the body of Christ. Another Global Scholars academic, Thomas K. Johnson, who taught at Charles University in Prague for many years, became one of the most respected theologians in the European church and is now the senior theological advisor to the World Evangelical Alliance. In November 2023, he was one of the key speakers at the international G-20 Religion Forum in Bali. Johnson's work at a public university helped prepare him to represent the worldwide evangelical community in that forum and others.

Serving the Community

I have helped to create an organization that provides mobility to polio survivors. We have built and distributed over twenty-eight thousand tricycle-type wheelchairs in the last twenty years. I have helped to create programs and write materials for national organizations that promote ethics in society. I have also helped to create two peacemaking organizations that have had a positive influence amid the violence in our city. On two occasions, I have fed and provided accommodation for dozens of internally displaced persons affected by local violence.

Serving the Government

Because we work in public universities, we are often invited to assist and participate in government functions. I have been invited on government radio and television as an expert to discuss issues such as violence, education, and Christian ministry. I have helped to develop in-service programs for thousands of public-school teachers. I instigated the creation of a set of six manuals for teachers of Christian Religious Education in Nigeria's public schools. I have led in the development of an organization that worked closely with the Ministries of Health and Education to develop faith-based approaches to the HIV/AIDS issue that have been used in every

Nigerian state. We have received hundreds of thousands of dollars from the Nigerian government to develop and implement these faith-based training programs. We are now using our experiences with HIV to address the growing substance abuse problem in Nigeria. On two occasions, I have preached before Nigeria's president and other government officials at the presidential villa chapel. Politicians look good when they solve problems, so when government officials learn you have something to contribute to nation-building, they often come looking for you.

Christian academics have particularly promising opportunities in African public universities, for several reasons. First, all universities in Anglophone Africa use English as an official language. Therefore, academics from North America do not have to learn a second language to teach there. Second, Anglophone Africa has been less influenced by secularism than Western institutions, so one can talk freely about faith. Third, many African countries look to the West for assistance, including scholars for their universities. This vacuum is one Christian academics can fill. Fourth, because most African countries are developing countries, Christian academics can engage more in nation-building and social and moral change than in more advanced countries.

Teaching in a Public University Is Good

Personal Development

God has designed us to continually grow and develop. No other profession in the world stimulates growth better than teaching in a public university. Academics interact with key people in society. They are exposed to the arts, culture, and intellectual life. This helps instructors develop a holistic perspective on life.

Career

Academics do three things that help them develop a well-rounded and fulfilling career. They teach, conduct research, and serve as administrators. Although I have been able to focus specifically on my primary discipline of New Testament theology, I have taught twenty-six different courses at the University of Jos.

Over the last fifteen years, I have led major research projects on Pentecostalism, religious freedom, the perception of leprosy, HIV/AIDS, and the use of language in the church. These projects have received substantial funding from different foundations and have collaborated with the University of Southern California, Georgetown University, and Emory University.

Regarding administration, in my first few years of university service, I coordinated the Diploma in Christian Studies program. I have also served as member and chair of several committees. The most interesting of these committees was created by the university senate because so many people were becoming believers and making restitution to the university for cheating during their student days. I served as the founding chairman of the Committee on Restitution, Confession, and Forgiveness. In 2020, I was appointed as the director of the Centre for Conflict Management and Peace Studies, which was created in 2002 to address the chaos and violence central Nigeria has experienced. Our center offers three academic programs, participates in research, and engages in interventions.

If you become a lifelong academic, you will develop a career and ministry that is unique, challenging, and fulfilling.

Family

One thing that attracted me to international ministry was my admiration for the children of a Christian scholar who served as a missionary in Korea. I wanted my children to experience similar things. After raising my children in Africa, I am even more convinced that international service, particularly in a public university has many advantages for one's family. It exposes your family to other parts of the world. My children have traveled far more than most of their cousins. It also helps make your children mature and fulfilled adults. Traveling and interacting extensively with people in the international community help to create a healthy and well-rounded worldview.

International life also opens up career opportunities for your children. My oldest daughter has a PhD in African languages and literature and teaches at the prestigious School of Oriental and Africa Studies (SOAS) in the University of London. My son lives in Lagos, Nigeria and has a video business that takes him all over Africa. He has conducted interviews with heads of state and major international leaders, and won Emmys, and other international awards for his work. My youngest daughter, a physician and Lieutenant Commander in the U.S. Navy, has traveled all over the world, flown F-18s off aircraft carriers, and jumped out of airplanes with the Navy Seals. I believe my career of teaching at African public universities has been good for my children.

Teaching in a Public University Is Required

To Obey the Great Commission

Jesus told his disciples, "Go and make disciples of all nations" (Matt 28:19 NIV). Universities are found in all nations. A great way to influence those nations is to become a *bona fide* academic.

To Be Salt and Light in the World

Jesus said, "You are the salt of the earth … you are the light of the world" (Matt 5:13–14 NIV). These figures of speech suggest that we must live and work in every part of society if we are to build God's kingdom in every part of society. The university is a strategic part of the world. If we are to fulfill Jesus's expectations, we must be part of the world's public universities.

To Make Christ Lord over Every Part of the World

Paul said, "At the name of Jesus every knee should bow, in heaven and on earth and under the earth, and every tongue acknowledge that Jesus Christ is Lord" (Phil 2:10–11 NIV). "Every knee" and "every tongue" includes those knees and tongues found in public universities.

Conclusion

Two famous men were greatly influenced by public universities. First, John Wesley joined with his brother Charles to initiate a "holy club" while attending Oxford University. Though his "heart-warming" experience came later, the discipline, piety, and accountability he learned at Oxford helped to shape his life and ministry. Wesley's enormous impact on evangelicalism and global missions which have impacted millions was greatly enhanced at a public university.

The second man went to a university as a rather casual believer. However, at King Abdulaziz University in Jeddah, Saudi Arabia, Osama bin Laden met a professor who radically changed his life and ours, by inspiring him to pursue a radical form of Islam. What if bin Laden had met and been influenced by a Christian professor instead?

Lecturing at a public university is not for everyone. It takes many years of tedious study to be qualified, and it certainly offers many challenges. However, I cannot think of a more fulfilling and potentially influential way to build God's kingdom than serving God in a public university.

Bibliography

Global Scholars. Accessed February 15, 2023. www.global-scholars.org.

Henderson, Roger. "Kuyper's Inch." *Pro Rege* 36, no. 3 (2008): 12–14. https://digitalcollections.dordt.edu/pro_rege/vol36/iss3/2.

Leuner, H. D. "Judaism." In *The World's Religions*. Edited by Norman Anderson. Grand Rapids, MI: Eerdmans, 1983.

Further Reading

Gould, Paul, M. "The Outrageous Idea of a Missional Professor." *International Edition*. Eugene, OR: Wipf & Stock, 2019.

Lingenfelter, Judith, and Sherwood G. Lingenfelter. *Teaching Cross-Culturally*. Grand Rapids, MI: Baker Academic, 2003.

Marsden, George M. *The Outrageous Idea of Christian Scholarship*. New York: Oxford Press, 1977.

Noll, Mark. *Jesus Christ and the Life of the Mind*. Grand Rapids, MI: Eerdmans, 2011.

Romanowski, Michael, and Terri McCarthy. *Teaching in a Distant Classroom*. Downers Grove, IL: IVP Books, 2009.

Part Three

Mission in Word—Discipleship and Training

The word of God is powerful not only for salvation (Rom 1:16 ESV), but for "teaching, for reproof, for correction, and for training in righteousness, that the man of God may be complete, equipped for every good work" (2 Tim 3:16–17 ESV). As those who work for God's global glory, we seek to follow God's command from 2 Timothy 2:15: "Do your best to present yourself to God as one approved … rightly handling the word of truth."

It is a relief to know that the Bible does not recognize a lone ranger style of discipleship—making disciples is an inherently interconnected process that involves "building up the body of Christ" (Eph 4:12 ESV) in community. The following section seeks to strengthen the global disciple-making community through the sharing of best practices from practitioners in diverse global contexts who have been deeply involved in discipleship ministries through Bible translation, theological education, and church planting.

Chapter 8

Experiencing the Adventure of Bible Translation

Ted B. Wingo

In God's grand storyboard, the translation of Scripture plays a vital role. From man's initial directive to fill the earth with God's image-bearers to its fulfillment in Revelation, God has spoken clearly to man in his word. The message and the method merged when his Son, the Word, became flesh and tabernacled among us (John 1:14). We were then sent on mission (John 20:21). After the Fall, the Flood, and Babel, God's will has been the same: restoring his original purpose and plan. Stated many ways throughout history, his mission tied to his promise has remained constant—blessing all the families of the earth; light shining to the nations; witnesses to the ends of the earth; worshipers, disciples, and faithful obedience of all peoples; loving God and loving neighbors.

God's will climaxes in worshipers (image-bearers) from every tribe, tongue, people, and nation filling the earth and then praising his Son around the throne! The image of tongues of fire (a symbol of God's presence to all languages) resting on the first believers filled with the Spirit at Pentecost is pregnant with meaning. The fact that God reversed Babel,[1] causing all to hear in their own language, is also prophetic. Christianity must not be confined to one language or culture. It is for all to embrace in their heart language. "No culture is so advanced and so superior that it can claim exclusive advantage to the truth of God."[2]

Beginning at Pentecost, the Word by the Spirit spread around the known world. At the close of the New Testament, John reminds us where all of history is headed—to a restored garden with God's image-bearers filling the new earth and worshiping his Son.

---
1 Smither, *Mission in the Way of Daniel*, 60.
2 Sanneh, *Disciples of All Nations*, 25.

We have seen God's word translated and spread by those with the vision of his image-bearers in every people group around the earth. Giants of the faith have labored to translate Scripture into clear, natural, and accurate language to spread his fame among all peoples. Men like Wulfila,[3] Jerome, Wycliffe, Luther, Tyndale, Carey, and others have undertaken this task. Any modern translator of God's word realizes he stands on the shoulders of giants who suffered much to bring that word to others.

The journey for my wife and me to translate some of the Bible into the Tarahumara language began in college. Because of the Great Commission, we were challenged to consider missions—unless we were called to *stay*. Besides receiving undergraduate degrees, we developed friendships during that time, and I learned skills (such as riding motorcycles and four-wheeling) that would prove handy for life in the mountains of northern Mexico. After five years serving in a church plant in the United States and completing seminary studies, we spent twenty-five years serving among the Tarahumara people of Mexico.

The Challenge of Translation

Translation is difficult work. Who hasn't seen the signs at airports or read instructions where someone with a limited understanding of a foreign language used a dictionary and, obviously, didn't consult a native speaker? Results can be strange, weird, or downright unintelligible:

- No Littering! Violators will be fine.
- Beware of safety!
- Eating carpet strictly prohibited.
- Because you are dangerous you must not enter!
- Execution in Progress!
- On a gas/oil company t-shirt: I have gas.

Through the years, I've made many of my own mistakes and blunders. Once, I visited a tribal leader who lived, at times, in a cave. As he graciously invited me into one of his humble abodes and asked if I would care to dip some water from a bucket with his cup (a floating half gourd), I declined, wanting to say I brought my own water. However, mixing up *buku* and *muku*, I answered his kind offer with, "No thank you, it will kill me."

---

3 Walls, *Missionary Movement*, 38.

Later, after I had begun some translation in the Old Testament, I discovered I had made a big mistake in translating "Pharaoh had a hard heart." Graciously, God gave me a perfect way to check the translation in context. I was out cutting wood with Miguel, and he asked me where my wife was. When I responded that she was home alone, he immediately exclaimed, "*We bewágame sulégame ju alué mukí!*" which literally meant "she has a hard heart." What he meant in context was that she was very brave, since a murderer was in the area at the time and people were afraid to be home alone! That conversation saved me from using a phrase that seemed literally correct but meant something totally different!

Another time, a colleague and I wrestled with translating "Son of Man," so we went with "*Pe apiépiri rió.*" It sounded pretty good *until* we checked with native speakers. What we wanted to communicate was "a son who was fully human." However, what the Tarahumara heard was that Mary had slept with so many men that she didn't know who her baby's father was!

I hope you are convinced by now that checking and double-checking for clear, accurate, and natural translation is critical. This process involves using good hermeneutics and exegesis to get to the meaning in the original Hebrew, Aramaic, and Greek. Culture, of course, also plays a huge role in extracting the meaning. God is a master communicator, and he connects with specific life situations.

Translating the Bible
Levels of meaning transferance
God's grand storyboard

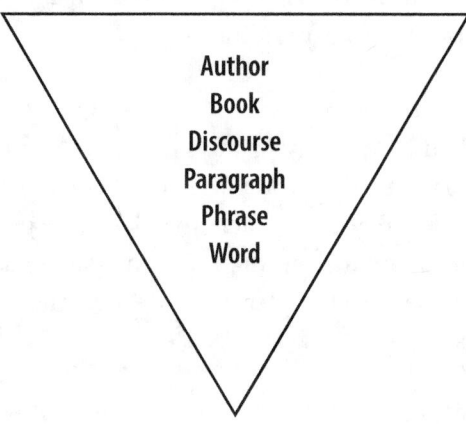

The Translation Process

In translation, we must seek to relate the message in a way that carries the same meaning and impact from the source to the receptor languages (see the previous diagram). The message of God in the Bible is important, from the over-arching metanarrative to the choice of individual words and tagmemes. The translation should sing and sting *with its original impact* in the receptor language. As we embark on the process of translation, we consider the biblical authors, books, discourse with Scripture, paragraphs, phrases, and individual words.

Authors

God communicated his message in the Bible through human authors uniquely chosen for each specific genre to record his word as they were inspired by the Spirit. As I progressed in my knowledge of Greek, I realized there was quite a difference in the authors' vocabulary and style. John, Paul, and Luke had unique approaches to how they conveyed their message. A translation should capture this diversity of style and not sound like it was written by a single person.

Books

An entire book of the Bible might be written in a way that conveys a message through its structure. One example is chiasm. In Romans, for example, the letter is bookended with the theme, "faithful obedience of all peoples" (1:5; 16:26). In the center of the book (chapter 8), this theme comes to a climax as believers who bear God's image fill a restored earth and worship the Lord. Worship (from individuals, groups, and from among all peoples) is a reasonable response to the gospel (Rom 12–15).[4]

Discourse

Discourse is handled in a variety of ways in different cultures. Translating Luke 15, the story of the prodigal son, helped me gain a deeper understanding of this reality. In fact, the deeper I got into translating God's word into Tarahumara and the more the people began to grasp the meaning, the more they began to teach me deeper truths as I saw the word through their eyes.

---

4 Piper, "Supremacy of God," 69.

Have you ever noticed that the only dialogue in the story of the prodigal son is between the father and the elder brother? Tarahumara noted that immediately—most likely because, in their discourses, they break into dialogue themselves for the climax or main theme of the story!

Paragraphs

Once I was checking a paragraph-length translation I realized how we all tend to supply information to a story from our experience. We were working through John 11 with our language consultant, Nacho. My colleague asked him what he pictured when hearing that the people were mourning at Lazarus's house. He promptly filled in the story, assuring her that they were offering food and drink to Lazarus's spirit to help his soul on the long journey to the afterlife. I quickly assured him that none of that was in the text! The experience demonstrates the need to be aware of the assumptions that cultural groups, including our own, bring to a passage and to be sure to communicate clearly in light of those assumptions.

Phrases

Genesis 4 includes a short but interesting phrase. Often translated as Eve saying, "*With the help of* the LORD I have brought forth a man," the italicized phrase is a translation of the particle or word, אֵת, in Hebrew. It can mean "with" or be a marker for apposition. In other words, Eve could have thought her firstborn was the promised one who would crush Satan's head, that is, the Lord! If true, this interpretation would mean that her expectation was right on, even if her timing was not.[5]

Word

At the level of individuals words, the simple pronoun "we" can cause quite a stir in languages that don't have a generic "we." Is the reference to an inclusive or exclusive "we"? For example, in Mark's Gospel Jesus is asleep in a boat. As the storm raged, the panic-stricken disciples woke Jesus and cried, "We're going to perish!" In languages without a generic "we," we must delineate if Jesus was included in the "we." Was Jesus also going to perish? The Greek text and biblical commentaries aren't much help. The translator must decide, using sound theology, hermeneutics, and exegesis arrive at a solid understanding of the passage in its context.

---

5 Kaiser, *Messiah in the Old*, 42.

The Transfer Model

```
    SL                              RL
(Source Language)            (Receptor Language)
                      TL
      Discover   (Transtor Language)   Re-express
    the meaning                         the meaning

                    Meaning
```

Language and Culture

The relationship between language and culture became very apparent to me as our translation team worked through the translation of John's Gospel. My colleague Carol pointed out that every time we worked through a large passage of Scripture, our language consultant, Nacho, gave a summary statement upfront *before* adding any details of the story itself. Understanding this tendency and applying it to translation and teaching helped us communicate the message—the big picture—in a way that the Tarahumara could more readily grasp. Without knowing beforehand that the metanarrative of Scripture was about a new kind of relationship with God through Christ, the Tarahumara often got lost in the details and ended up just adding some biblical facts to their existing worldview.

This tendency was also evident when we translated John 20:21, "As the Father has sent me, even so send I you." It was actually the next verse that unlocked the message of John and all of Scripture for Nacho. When Jesus gathered his disciples around Him, He blew on them. Nacho said: "Oh! This is what John is all about! Life! He came to give life; born-again life; living water; bread of life; resurrection life; life more abundant. Oh! This is what God did in the garden when he breathed into Adam's nose! He gave not just physical life but spirit life—the life that was lost when Adam sinned and that Jesus came to restore!"

Learning language and culture for translation is important, not just for the recipients, but also for Bible translators. Seeing the word through the eyes of new believers, we glimpse new aspects of the splendor of God's majesty and are able to more fully glorify him (Eph 3:10). In the Western church, we often believe we are okay as we are and don't need the rest of the world. Further, we often don't believe that those who have yet to hear the gospel might add something to our understanding of God and his word. In reality, we need believers from diverse parts of the globe to help us become aware of our own limited cultural perspectives.[6]

Conclusion

We went to the Tarahumara primarily to reach them. Yet, in living and sharing with them, we learned a lot about true life in Christ. They taught us how to break bread (*remé*) house to house and rejoice in life in Jesus. In their dance, we learned to celebrate the Spirit-breathed life that Jesus came to restore. And we learned that this life is to be shared at the deepest level as we worship God.

Translating God's Word into the Tarahumara language and into all languages is a "means to a much greater end—the glory of God among the nations, that the name of Jesus may be honored, loved, and obeyed and that his name may be renowned."[7]

Bibliography

Hiebert, Paul. "The Missionary as Mediator of Global Theologizing." In *Globalizing Theology*, edited by Craig Ott and Harold Netland, 288–308. Grand Rapids, MI: Baker Academic, 2006.

Kaiser, Walter C., Jr. *The Messiah in the Old Testament*. Grand Rapids, MI: Zondervan, 1995.

Metcalf, Sam. *Beyond the Local Church*. Downers Grove, IL: InterVarsity Press, 2015.

Piper, John. *Let the Nations Be Glad!: The Supremacy of God in Missions*. Grand Rapids, MI: Baker Books, 1993.

Piper, John. "The Supremacy of God in Missions through Worship." In *Discovering the Mission of God*, edited by Mike Barnett, 68–84. Downers Grove, IL: IVP Academic, 2012.

Plass, Ewald. *What Luther Says*. Saint Louis, MO: Concordia, 2006.

Richardson, Don. *Eternity in Their Hearts*. Ventura, CA: Regal, 1981.

Richardson, Steve. *Is the Commission Still Great?* Chicago: Moody Publishers, 2022.

Sanneh, Lamin. *Disciples of All Nations: Pillars of World Christianity*. New York: Oxford University Press, 2008.

---

6 Hiebert, "Missionary as Mediator," 907.

7 Metcalf, *Beyond the Local Church*, 206.

Schnabel, Eckhard. *Early Christian Mission: Paul and the Early Church*. Vol. 2. Downers Grove, IL: InterVarsity Press, 2004.

Smither, Edward L. *Mission in the Way of Daniel*. Littleton, CO: William Carey Publishing, 2022.

Walls, Andrew. *The Missionary Movement in Christian History*. Maryknoll, NY: Orbis, 2007.

Chapter 9
Informal Theological Education
The Case of Shepherds Global Classroom

Timothy Keep

The future of global mission must include informal theological education. Shepherds Global Classroom (SGC) exists to serve underserved pastors and Christian leaders around the world by providing a unique curriculum for the multiplication of indigenous, informal, and non-formal Bible schools and seminaries.

Our Story

In April 2012, I was traveling with other missionary trainers through East Africa, teaching a diverse group of pastors and laypeople in small villages and in very rustic settings. In each place, pastors and Christian leaders gathered under the shade of mango trees, simple make-shift shelters, or tents. It was a wonderful, eye-opening season of ministry. These men and women who had had almost no access to theological training were eager students. I was often amazed by their spiritual depth and insight, but also saddened by their lack of resources. And as we taught, it became evident that some of the pastors and leaders that we were training had the heart, capacity, and gifts to teach as well. They didn't really need us to teach them—they needed us to equip them to do what we were doing.

One beautiful morning in a village in Mozambique, I sat on the porch of a mission house with an open Bible before me. A salty breeze from the Indian Ocean rustled gently through the coconut palms, while a farmer cultivated his pineapple garden nearby. As I read John 13, I was struck by a phrase from the story of Jesus washing his disciples' feet: "Do you understand what I have done to you … *I have given you an example*, that you also should do just as I have done to you" (John 13:12, 15 ESV). As I pondered this word, the events of the past days, the men and women I'd been privileged to teach, and this strong desire God had given me to equip Christian leaders, the thought came to me that we could serve Jesus's disciples best by providing a training resource suited for them and for their context. *What if we had a training curriculum that was theologically robust, but simple, clear, and concise to put into the hands of these pastors?* That morning I sensed the Holy Spirit was saying that if we would find a way to develop this needed resource as a service to his diverse body, he would bless the effort.

Over the next few months, God affirmed this calling and providentially brought together a team of qualified, dedicated cross-cultural trainers and educators to begin the work. Within a year or so, this nameless vision became known as Shepherds Global Classroom, Inc. Since the planting of the first tiny seeds in 2012, hundreds of thousands of dollars have been invested into twenty foundational English courses and numerous translations. These courses are already equipping leaders to train men and women in thirty-seven countries for the harvest. Our free Shepherds Global Classroom App has been downloaded in ninety-one countries.

Global Theological Famine

According to the Global Alliance for Church Multiplication (GACX), "About four in every ten people are living in places where there are few to no believers or churches. Another 30 percent are in places the gospel has reached but they are still waiting to hear."[1] God desires that every person hear the good news, a desire which will only be fulfilled through the multiplication of "local, indigenous church(es) filled with equipped, fruitful disciples."[2] SGC strives to be an equipping arm of the church planting movement taking place around the world.

SGC exists because a vast majority of churches around the world are led by people who have no formal education in theology or ministry. Ramesh Richard states, "These pastors lack theological discernment, a strong undergirding of biblical spirituality, and a preaching method to communicate God's word in a faithful, deep, and compelling way."[3] According to David Livermore:

> There's little question that there's compelling need to serve the global church with theological and leadership training. The expansive growth of the church around the world is producing a shortage of theologically equipped pastors and church leaders.
>
> There are approximately 2.2 million evangelical churches in the world.

---

1 See GACX, "About."

2 GACX, "About."

3 RREACH, "Ministry Training."

85% are led by men and women who have no theological training.

7,000 new church leaders are needed daily to care for the growing church.

If every Christian training institute in the world operated at 120% capacity, less than 10% of the unequipped leaders would be trained.[4]

Our South African friends at Re-forma add: "The biggest crisis facing the evangelical, global church today is the fact that most pastors, missionaries, and Christian leaders are undertrained or not trained at all."[5] Shepherds Global Classroom strives to respond to this crisis.

A lack of discipleship and theological training makes the global church susceptible to deception and false teaching. In twenty-seven years of missionary service, I've witnessed so much real-world pain and suffering brought on by the absence of careful biblical instruction.

I remember visiting a village in the Philippines with several pastors where we met a dear lady with a painful skin disease covering her entire body. She and her family were believers with little biblical knowledge. We learned that they had spent lots of money on doctors to no avail. Finally, they went to see a prosperity gospel evangelist passing through their city. They gave their "seed offering," which impoverished them even more, and tried their best to believe God for healing but nothing happened. In the little time there, we did our best to gently guide this family toward a more biblical understanding of divine healing. We laid our hands on the lady and prayed for healing according to James 5:14–15. We sensed God's love and compassion working through our team and from that moment she began to recover! SGC cares about biblically-based sound teaching for the global church.

The Mission of Shepherds Global Classroom

Given our vision to equip the body of Christ by providing curriculum for rising Christian leaders around the world, we envision homes, sanctuaries, cafes, and even shade trees as "classrooms" where underserved Christian leaders will be discipled and sent into the harvest. In recent years, Uber and Airbnb have radically transformed the taxi and hotel paradigm. They have scaled both by making use of private vehicles and homes. The SGC team believes we can do something similar—scaling indigenous theological classrooms—by tapping into the gifts and resources already present within the body of Christ around the world.

At the heart of the SGC mission is the unique curriculum tool—a theological curriculum which is Christ-centered, adaptable to various

---

4 Livermore, "American or American't," 456.

5 Re-Forma, "Home."

contexts, and makes training reproducible. We feel that this curriculum is unique and useful for the following reasons.

How It Is Written

SGC curriculum is biblically and theologically rich but also written in clear, simple language, especially those whose first language is not English. Each course has been developed by qualified and experienced cross-cultural leaders who have a passion for God's word. Textbooks are available in e-format while tests and answer keys are provided. Courses are full of illustrations, stories, quotes, character sketches, dialogue, maps, charts, and timelines. Each course is practical in nature and designed for those already in ministry. They are fully available for download from the Shepherds Global Classroom website or accessible through the SGC app.

What It Provides

SGC curriculum includes twenty foundational courses, covering a broad range of biblical theology. Courses are delivered in fifteen-week periods of time and the entire program can be completed in two to three years. Though we are not a training institution (i.e., Bible college), we provide excellent training materials that would allow informal training institutions to be birthed. The curriculum's structure makes it possible for courses to fit into most any context.

Shepherds Global Classroom Courses	
Exploring the Old Testament	The Christian Family
Exploring the New Testament	The Life and Ministry of Jesus
Principles of Biblical Interpretation	Ministry Leadership
Christian Beliefs	Principles of Communication
Romans	Introduction to Apologetics
Doctrine and Practice of the Holy Life	World Religions and Cults
Doctrine and Practice of the Church	Survey of Church History I
Biblical Evangelism and Discipleship	Survey of Church History II
Spiritual Formation	Introduction to Christian Worship
Practical Christian Living	Eschatology

Available in Translation

We began translating the curriculum into languages representing some of the world's greatest populations. As of January 2023, 156 courses have been translated with 113 others in progress.

Evangelical Unity

SGC values evangelical unity in its approach to theological training. We desire to serve the global body of Christ. We affirm the well-known saying, "In essentials unity, in non-essentials liberty, and in all things charity." Our motto is "Christ-centered. Training. Everywhere."

Equipping Trainers

SGC scales up theological training by equipping local Christian leaders, pastors, and missionaries as trainers who then form their own grassroots training programs. Through SGC, Christian leaders are being prepared as pastors, teachers, and ordained elders.

Free and Available

SGC offers all digital curriculum to trainers around the world for free through our web page or app. We grant printing and distribution rights to anyone. SGC does not charge royalty or membership fees when denominations, agencies, institutions, or individuals download and distribute SGC curriculum within their ministry. Access to a particular language file is available simply by contacting us.

Certificates from Partners

Though the training is free and accessible, global pastors and other students often like to receive a certificate for their work. Two recognized schools in the United States (Columbia International University and God's Bible School & College) partner with us to provide a certificate for those who complete the SGC program of study.

Training Consulting

Our team provides trainers to equip others to teach the SGC curriculum. At present, we are developing a network of trainers around the world, whom we serve by providing regular, online coaching. We are happy to expand this service upon request.

Feedback from the Field

Papua New Guinea

On a recent trip to Papua New Guinea, I received some unexpected encouragement from Pastor Roger, a brother in his early forties. As we slowly ascended a mountain road just outside of Mt. Hagen (in the back of a Toyota 4x4), he said, "SGC has changed my life ... Thank you for your ministry." Roger explained that though he had been pastoring for many years, he never had the opportunity to attend Bible college. Then a missionary named Shirley began offering Saturday classes (using SGC curriculum), and he eagerly enrolled. "Every Saturday, I've traveled four hours one way from my village to study with the group ... I've already completed fifteen SGC courses, and these courses have taught me so much."

Mexico

In Mexico, missionary Brennan Muir writes:

> SGC was instrumental in helping us to start Ezra Biblical Seminary. Since 2019, attendees have included pastors, church leaders, laypersons, and professionals. As we have grown from only a few students to more than sixty, we have seen the value of SGC for making disciples of Christ, no matter the level of one's education.

Ezra is now training students in six Central American countries.

Kenya

In Kenya, Pastor Silas discovered our courses online in 2017 and began training a group of leaders each week. For five years, they have continued this training program and have sent trainers to surrounding East African countries, including Malawi, Mozambique, Angola, South Sudan, Zambia, Uganda, and Tanzania.

Uganda

Eli Fader, a missionary in Uganda, states: "Northern Uganda is a strategic place for pastoral training right now. Many of the pastors in this area have not had the opportunity to study the word of God, and yet they faithfully serve their communities of believers." Eli and his wife Bethany serve in the refugee camps where the South Sudanese have fled their war-torn country. They are using SGC to train fifty church leaders each week who are returning to their own congregations to teach what they have learned.

Conclusion: A Biblical Mandate for Training

In Acts 8:26–32, Philip is called by God to leave Samaria and travel along a certain road near Gaza. There, he encountered a man from Ethiopia sitting in his chariot and reading from the prophet Isaiah. "Do you understand what you're reading?" Philip asked. The man responded, "How can I, unless someone guides me?" (vv. 30–31). *How can I, unless someone guides me?* This sentence has been very convicting to me. The Holy Spirit was doing supernatural things in those days, but when it came to a man who needed biblical understanding, he sent a teacher. This is God's normal response. At Shepherds Global Classroom, we see our curriculum, in the hands of trainers, as a kind of scalable teacher helping and guiding men and women into truth. SGC, then, is a practical response to the biblical mandate, "what you have heard from me in the presence of many witnesses entrust to faithful men, who will be able to teach others also" (2 Tim 2:2 ESV). In short, we strive to scale biblical training and to equip underserved pastors and rising leaders in the developing world.

Bibliography

GACX. "About." Accessed January 14, 2023. https://gacx.io/about.

Klett, Leah MarieAnn. "WEA Head: Biblical Illiteracy 'Utmost Problem' Facing Global Evangelicalism." *The Christian Post*, December 3, 2020. https://www.christianpost.com/news/wea-head-biblical-illiteracy-utmost-problem-facing-church.html.

Livermore, David. "American or American't: A Critical Analysis of Western Training to the World." *Evangelical Missions Quarterly* 40, no. 4 (Oct 2004): 456.

Livermore, David. *Serving with Eyes Wide Open: Doing Short-Term Missions with Cultural Intelligence*. Grand Rapids, MI: Baker Books, 2006.

Re-Forma. "Home." Accessed January 14, 2023. https://www.re-forma.global.

RREACH. "Ministry Training." Accessed January 14, 2023. https://rreach.org/reach-home-page/ministry-training/.

Chapter 10

Critical Shifts

Lessons in Church Planting in Europe

Dietrich Schindler

To grasp what challenges the North American evangelical church will face in the next ten years, one should look no further than post-Christian, secular Europe.[1] The European church planting context is unique. Secular society in Europe is largely made up of people who are either indifferent or hostile to the gospel. In many places, people have forgotten that they have forgotten God. Contemporary Europe is an unbelieving continent with a Christian residue.

Yet church planting is thriving in Europe. In the next ten years, ten thousand new churches will be planted in England, mostly through the Anglican Church. French Assembly of God churches are working toward generating one thousand new churches in ten years. In Germany, we are collaborating to see the number of newly planted churches double by 2032.

What approaches have church planters found that God has uniquely blessed? Based on my experience in Germany and Europe more broadly, I present multiple distinct shifts in church planting that can inform the global church and help it pivot to more effective church-planting methods, especially in secular contexts.

Shift from Organizational to Organic

All church plants in the New Testament were conversion-based. People like Lydia (Acts 16:11–40) or Cornelius (Acts 10) came to faith in Christ along with many in their relational networks (*oikos*) which resulted in the birth of new churches. In the modern Western world, we can tend to plant churches organizationally, not organically. Church planting ventures often follow a business plan approach. As such, the church planter and his team need to control the process, be highly visible, be well-trained theologically, and rely on the persona of a gifted leader.

---

1 These insights are taken from my book, *SHIFT: The Road to Level 5 Church Multiplication*.

The organizational approach, however, is fraught with problems. It is inherently high on control and low on risk. As such, it tends to domesticate God, putting him in the box of conventionality, expecting him to work along preconceived lines. The default mode of leadership is pastoral when it ought to be missional.

In Europe, we have seen fledgling examples of churches where evangelism preceded church planting. In the organizational model, church planting is seen as the vehicle for evangelism, not as its engine. Conversion-based churches have evangelism and missional behavior baked into their DNA.

The Evangelical Free Church in Lüneburg (northern Germany) started after an unusually large number of people trusted Jesus during an evangelistic tent campaign. A church in Stockerau, Austria, was birthed by the conversions of twenty people through a MyLife Workshop. In Berlin, Marcus Rose (Hoffnung Deutschland) has been able to generate literally hundreds of house churches with newly converted people meeting in bars and clubs.

Shift from Big to Small

When God wants to do something grand, he starts small. From one man, Abram, God promised to bless all the nations of the earth (Gen 12:1–3). Jesus said, the kingdom of God, is like a small mustard seed that grows into a huge tree (Matt 13:31–32). To feed five thousand people, Jesus began with five loaves and two pieces of fish (Luke 9:16–17). To disciple the whole world, Jesus invested three years of his life predominantly in the lives of twelve men. God loves small beginnings, and so should we.

In Germany, we have been starting "mini-churches." These are small groups of three "FAT" believers (faithful, available, teachable), always gender-specific; men with men, women with women. Together they practice spiritual breathing. They inhale, reading one chapter of the Bible daily. They gather once a week and share how God has been speaking to them in his word. At that meeting, they exhale, telling one another how they actually lived during the past seven days. They discuss four questions:

1. Where were you tempted, and how did you respond to the temptation?
2. Did you secretly serve someone without getting caught and without talking about it?
3. Were you angry with someone, and did you remain angry?
4. Did you give the people closest to you priority time?

After meeting together for one month, the group of three invites a fourth person—a non-Christian—into their group. The not-yet-believer is invited to do what the believers have been doing but just for two weeks since they may be hesitant to be transparent. Two weeks is a good time frame for a non-Christian to get a taste of the goodness of community. From start to finish, the shelf life of a mini-church is four months. Each group of four divides after four months into two groups of two, each adding another FAT Christian. Then the process starts all over again.

If someone has started a mini-church three times, we have just discovered our next church planter. They have proven on a small scale that they can shepherd a reproduction process. We then cluster groups of mini-churches in a given geographical location and generate a new church. The beauty of the mini-churches is that they are leaderless in structure. All one needs to do is to invite others into the process. Beyond that, these groups both disciple Christians and evangelize in one simple model.

Shift from Cognition to Emotion

One would think that since the culture is predominantly intellectual, a cognitive-based apologetic would work best in Europe. Interestingly, the very relationship focused Alpha Course has been connecting with many over the years. We are, however, noticing a decrease in its appeal to non-Christians. To invite a secular person to an Alpha Course, one must convince her that she should be interested in questions that do not interest her—who is Jesus? Is the Bible true? Is Christianity relevant?

What does interest a non-Christian is their own life. Ten years ago, the Lord led me to write and field test a new approach to reaching the heart of the secular person in Europe. The MyLife Workshop has been conducted over one thousand times in Europe in sixteen languages. We have seen one in four participants surrender their lives to Christ. What makes the course so unique is that it is emotion-based. At tables of four to five people, participants open up about the people and events that have both positively and painfully shaped them to become who they are. They share their stories, delving deeply into their aspirations and desires. In the process they see the gospel emerge out of their own life story.

One woman who came to faith in a MyLife Workshop said, "These six weeks have meant more to me than twenty years of therapy." A young man spoke of the course being the first time in his life where he learned to reflect on his past. He has since trusted in Jesus Christ. A German woman was so moved that she has started to pray regularly with her husband, saying, "Only God can help us."

Timothy Keller has said, "Christianity needs to make emotional sense before it can make rational sense."[2] The MyLife Workshop is making emotional sense of the gospel for many people in Europe today.

Shift from Membership to Discipleship

Jesus taught us not to make members but to make disciples. Dallas Willard laments, "So far as the visible Christian institutions of our day are concerned, *discipleship clearly is optional* (emphasis mine)."[3]

When the Lord calls us to the grand and glorious ministry of church planting, he calls us to make disciples, not simply members or visitors. He calls us to challenge those both within and still outside of the kingdom of God to leave their small worlds and to lay hold of the gospel. We are called to teach and preach a message that's as compelling as it is honest—to die to self and live unto Christ.

Healthy church planting will aim not at membership, but at followership. It will instill in people's hearts a vision of strength and beauty found only in Jesus Christ. A vision like this motivates people to turn from ordering their own lives and instead be reformatted by Christ and the word of God. This shift is so transformative that people will begin to see our love for God and for them. When they see such transformed lives, they'll begin to glimpse what Jesus looks like and long for him.

Shift from Go to Stop

The best gift we can give our church-planting ministry is the gift of a healthy soul. Every wholesome outcome begins with a healthy source. On the other hand, bad fruit comes from a bad root. If we want healthy, thriving, and life-giving church-planting ministries, we need to be leaders who are also healthy, thriving, and life-giving.

Church planters often live with a long to-do list—a myriad of things we need and want to accomplish. What we need most, however, is to start a stop-doing list of the things that will hinder us from pursuing greater depth and intimacy in our lives.

No church-planting venture will be more spiritually vibrant than the life of its leaders. Followers take their cues from those leading them. Ultimately, great church-planting ministries are not about methods, communication, strategy, or even fruit. They are born from those whose inner life and relationships are full of integrity.

---

2 Keller, "Emotion Isn't the Caboose" (Interview).

3 Dallas Willard, *Great Omission*, 4.

Shift from Town to Region

Roland Allen wrote: "In little more than ten years, Saint Paul established the church in four provinces of the Empire: Galatia, Macedonia, Achaia, and Asia. Before AD 47, there were no churches in these provinces; in AD 57, Saint Paul could speak as if his work there was done."[4] Roughly half of the references to newly planted churches in the New Testament point to the individual cities in which the churches were planted, such as Antioch, Corinth, Rome, and Ephesus. The other half speak of *regions* that were covered by church plants, such as Galatia, Macedonia, Achaia, and Asia.

When Jesus and his disciples went out preaching the good news of the kingdom of God, they were focusing their ministry regionally. The Jewish historian Josephus estimated that three million people lived in this northern region of Israel.[5] Jesus ministered in towns, cities, and villages with the goal of reaching the entire region of Galilee.

Our local church-planting ministries today often come at the cost of the region around those localities. The vision we have for our town or city can keep us from seeing our region. In 1990 in Bonn, Germany, only one Evangelical Free Church existed. In the next five years, between 1990 and 1995, this church doubled its membership, worship attendance, and more than doubled its number of small groups. This amazing growth was accompanied by the planting of new churches in the region around Bonn. Every year for five consecutive years, the Evangelical Free Church of Bonn planted a new church. Today, the combined attendance of all these churches is three times that of the mother church.

If we never move from where we are, we will never move to where God wants us to go. This is a basic tenet of movement. If we want to start more than one church and have a broader and wider impact, we should move away from focusing solely on one church planting locale.

Shift from Addition to Multiplication

In 2001, the business world awakened to a new benchmark when Jim Collins published his provocative findings in his best-selling book, *Good to Great*. Supported by a large research team, Collins identified companies that made

---

4 Allen, *Missionary Methods*, 3.

5 In *Vita*, par 45, Josephus writes of two hundred forty towns and villages in Galilee. In *Bellum* III, iii. 2, he writes that the smallest of these villages had more than fifteen thousand residents. We can thus calculate that according to Josephus, the region of Galilee had a population of more than three million people.

the jump from good results to great results and sustained those results for fifteen years or more. What he discovered was that good companies had been lulled into doing business as usual, while great companies excelled in the areas of personnel appropriation, reality checks, and "transcending the curse of competence, cultural discipline, and technology acceleration."[6] Collins' findings riveted the attention of many and made the book into a long-standing best-seller.

What surprised Collins was not the enthusiastic reception his work received from the business community, but rather from members of the non-profit sector. One-third of his readers worked in social occupations and they were most eager to apply his principles to their setting. Collins obliged the hunger of the non-profit community for greater clarity by writing a supplemental monograph on how *Good to Great* principles could be carried over to the social sectors.[7]

The imagery of "good to great" also applies to church planting. Stellar church-planting churches bear down on specific disciplines that infuse their ministries with remarkable movement-based energy, vision, and effectiveness. In my thirty years of church-planting experience in Germany, I have come to refer to seven disciplines of "good to great" church planting as "G7."[8] Based on my observation, great church-planting ministries seem to have seven qualities that set them apart from merely good church-planting ministries. These seven qualities of great church planting are:

- Timed Release: What is date for the next church-plant?
- Generational Distance: Instead of counting mother-daughter church plants, count the generations spawned from the mother-church.
- Discipleship Depth: Beyond simply believing in Jesus, focus on becoming more like Jesus.
- Intentional Mindset: Multiplication must be an intentional and unabated focus.
- External focus: The future of Jesus's movement lies in the harvest field and not in the barn.

---

6 Collins, *Good to Great*, 13.

7 Collins, *Good to Great*.

8 See a further discussion of this in Schindler, "Good to Great Church Planting," 330–37.

- Reproducible Models: Use a model for evangelism and discipleship that functions well whether official leaders or evangelists are present or not.
- Multiplication Coordinator: The church has a person who has the bird's eye view of church planting gestation periods and keeps church-plants on target.

Conclusion

Instead of only going to North America, Africa, or Asia for the next big idea to foster better church planting, why not look to Europe as well? God is doing new and exciting things on the Old Continent. Those of us who know him and want to partner with him by making him known by planting new churches can gain fresh perspective and encouragement by looking at what God is doing in Europe.

Bibliography

Allen, Roland. *Missionary Methods: St. Paul's or Ours?* Grand Rapids, MI: Eerdmans, 1993.

Collins, Jim. *Good to Great and the Social Sectors: Why Business Thinking is Not the Answer*. New York: Harper Business, 2005.

Collins, Jim. *Good to Great: Why Some Companies Make the Leap and Others Don't*. New York: Harper Business, 2001.

Josephus, Flavius. *The Life and Works of Flavius Josephus*. Translated by William Whiston. Philadelphia: John C. Winston, 1957.

Keller, Tim. "Emotion Isn't the Caboose to Faith." Interview by Owen Strachan. *Christianity Today*, May 30, 2014. Online: https://www.christianitytoday.com/ct/2014/april-web-only/jesus-resonates-with-people.html.

Schindler, Dietrich. "Good to Great Church Planting: The Road Less Traveled." *Evangelical Missions Quarterly* 44, no. 3 (July 2008): 330–37.

Schindler, Dietrich. *Shift: The Road to Level 5 Church Multiplication*. Orlando: Exponential, 2021.

Willard, Dallas. *The Great Omission: Reclaiming Jesus' Essential Teachings on Discipleship*. San Francisco: Harper, 2006.

Chapter 11

Coaching Church Planters in Central Europe, Russia, and Central Asia

Rick Amos

In this chapter, I explore how to inject coaching DNA into church-planting movements in secular cultures that often lack an ethos for mentoring and discipleship. I will present case studies from indigenous movements that have successfully created and maintained coaching relationships for pastors and women's ministry leaders. My aim is to help Christian church leaders who are responsible for developing spiritual leaders in churches, church-planting movements, and parachurch organizations.

I am a US citizen who has served in Central Europe, Russia, and Central Asia for almost thirty years. The wave of Western missionaries in the 1990s and 2000s brought energy, education, and finances to the beleaguered Protestant churches in this region of the world. While church growth during these years was significant, there were gaps in effective leadership development. The following observations and suggestions come from what I've learned during many hours of coaching conversations with indigenous church leaders.

Challenges for Leadership Development

Consider these scenarios.

- A pastor in Ukraine has a passion for evangelism but struggles to connect relationally as a preacher, disciple maker, and care giver. He grew up in an orphanage and although he had excellent seminary education, his low emotional intelligence is a barrier to his effectiveness as a pastor.
- A children's ministry leader in Belarus loves children, but her legalistic upbringing as a pastor's daughter causes her to rule the children with an iron hand and chase away volunteers with many rules and shame-based motivation. The gospel of grace has never penetrated her heart.

- A pastor and movement leader is a talented preacher and motivational leader. Other pastors are attracted to him, but because of insecurities from an abusive father, he remains aloof emotionally and never admits weaknesses or mistakes to even his closest colleagues. He has not dealt with the brokenness from his family of origin.
- A pastor in Russia attended seminary in his own country and got advanced degrees from an American seminary. He has a robust education, but has no skills in leading teams, resolving conflicts, managing administration, or interacting with other pastors with different theology.
- A women's ministry leader in Albania feels the constant pressure for perfection as a pastor's wife but longs to see women in her community come to faith in Christ and be discipled to maturity. The lack of support from the elders (including her husband) and the lack of friendship with other pastors' wives or women in ministry causes her to give up her dream and retreat to working full-time in an unsatisfying job to support her family.
- A pastor received a significant donation from Western partners to help build a church building. The cash sat in a safe in his home until one day he "borrowed" the funds to start a business venture that eventually failed. The pastor left his ministry in disgrace, the funds were never returned, and the church members struggled to trust the new leadership.

These are just some of the sad stories from leaders in Central Europe, Russia, and Central Asia. How did these gaps in spiritual maturity occur? How could these leaders have experienced greater development? What changes in organizational culture or education or training could help to combat these challenges? Today many church leaders in this region are seeing significant leadership development among young leaders through an intentional commitment to relational transparency and the application of coaching techniques in discipleship.

The Goal of Spiritual Maturity

Leaders learn to begin with the end in mind. What leadership development objectives are we looking for? The goal is spiritual maturity. The Apostle Paul expresses this overall aim with characteristic passion: "Him we proclaim, warning everyone and teaching everyone with all wisdom, that we may present everyone mature in Christ. For this I toil, struggling with all his energy that he powerfully works within me" (Col 1:28–29 ESV).

What do we see in this passage?

- "Him we proclaim"—the gospel is the focus for salvation, sanctification, and development.
- "Everyone"—we warn, teach, and present the whole body of Christ.
- "Mature in Christ"—this is the ultimate goal.
- "Toil" and "struggling"—it takes human effort to bring others to maturity.
- "His energy"—it requires divine power from the Holy Spirit to see the fruit of maturity in others.

No one would disagree that spiritual maturity is an important goal. The challenge is to align education, conferences, training, literature, and other developmental strategies toward this aim.

Years ago, I was an elder at a local church and we needed greater clarity for our plan for spiritual maturity among our members. I took a summer to study New Testament Greek words that described different phases of spiritual maturity. We embraced this list as we strove to "present everyone mature in Christ":

- Unbeliever
- New Believer
- Disciple on Mission
- Disciple Maker
- Group Leader or Ministry Leader
- Deacon or Elder
- Pastor
- Missionary Pastor

If you are a pastor or movement leader or women's ministry leader, develop your own milestones for Christian maturity and align your developmental strategies with your desired outcomes.

If you are a movement leader, extend this approach to include the leadership roles that are necessary to lead your movement, including:

- Pastor Coach—to be able to invest in younger pastors.
- Women's Ministry Coach—to assist women's ministry leaders in local churches.
- Movement Specialist—for evangelism, discipleship, preaching, and administration.

- Movement Leader—to serve on the leadership team.
- Movement Director—to lead the movement.
- Movement Missionary—to go and start a new church-planting movement.

Creating a Culture of Transparent Relationships

Dietrich Schindler says, "Spiritual growth requires transparency, openness, and accountability."[1] In an intensely personal letter, the Apostle Paul bares his soul and reminds believers how his team shared their very lives with the people: "But we were gentle among you, like a nursing mother taking care of her own children. So, being affectionately desirous of you, we were ready to share with you not only the gospel of God but also our own selves, because you had become very dear to us" (1 Thess 2:7–8 ESV). He continues, "For you know how, like a father with his children, we exhorted each one of you and encouraged you and charged you to walk in a manner worthy of God, who calls you into his own kingdom and glory" (1 Thess 2:11–12 ESV). Education without relationship is information. Discipleship without transparency is indoctrination. Mentoring without humility brings shame and withdrawal.

If you are a disciple maker, mentor, church leader, or movement leader, how can you create a culture of relational transparency? It begins with you as you live the gospel in humility. Sometimes it means confessing your sins to those you lead. It always requires recognizing that you are on the journey toward maturity instead of implying that you have already arrived.

Many missionaries moved their families to this region of the world, learned the language and culture, reached out to unbelievers who found faith in Christ, discipled new believers, and raised up leaders for the church. They did more than educate; they shared their very lives with indigenous believers.

As I walk with indigenous leaders, they often reflect on the men and women who invested in them. They almost never speak of theology learned or church growth strategies explained. They talk about how these foreigners struggled to speak their language, how they loved their spouses, how they parented their children, drove their cars, played sports, how they admitted their mistakes and strove to learn and grow. It has not been easy for these national leaders to build transparency into their own cultural relationships, but they often think back to the missionaries who set this powerful example for them.

---

1 Schindler, Presentation at Columbia International University, 2022.

Using a "Coach Approach" in Leadership Development

Solomon writes, "The purposes of a person's heart are deep waters, but one who has insight draws them out" (Prov 20:5 NIV). The Bible speaks of the value of teachers, advisors, older men, older women, mentors, and others who instruct, give advice, and share wisdom. This kind of input is critically important for leadership development. However, this verse speaks about another kind of helper—a coach who does not pour into someone, but rather "draws out" the deep waters of a person's heart.

The concept of coaching has developed significantly over the last thirty-five years. Sometimes a leader needs to be a *commander* who tells his team what to do during a crisis. Sometimes they need to be a *consultant* when the team lacks skills or experience. Other times, a leader needs to be a *counselor* who helps teammates to find healing for wounds or help amid challenges. However, most of the time, a leader ought to be a *coach* who comes alongside his team and "draws out" of them what they need to discover for themselves. This approach results in great motivation for growth and achievement.

What Is a Coach?

A coach is not an expert retained to give advice. They're not a teacher hired for instruction. Nor are they a counselor or therapist who assists a hurting person through the process of healing. A coach is not even a mentor—one who imparts spiritual knowledge.

So what is true coaching? Keith Webb asserts: "Coaching involves listening to others, asking questions to deepen thinking, allowing others to find their own solutions and doing it all in a way that makes people feel empowered and responsible enough to take action."[2] Indeed, listening is critical to coaching—listening to what is said but also what is conveyed non-verbally through body language. Asking good questions is also essential for helping someone move forward. When a coach allows others to find their own solutions, those disciples experience more ownership of their lives and become more motivated for change—much more than if they had simply been given advice. In fact, in a coaching conversation, advice is rarely given. Terri Amos adds, "Christian coaching recognizes that the Holy Spirit guides and directs a believer. A Christian coach assists someone in the discovery of God's leading in their lives, trusting the Holy Spirit who is at work inside of them."[3]

---

2 Webb, *Coach Model for Christian*, 19.

3 Amos, *Women in Ministry*, 2022.

Listening and Asking Questions

How do we listen well as coaches? Instead of offering lots of advice, what if we asked clear questions such as:

- What happened?
- How did you feel? What else?
- What does this mean for you? What else?
- How is that important for you? What else?
- What do you think God is doing in this situation? What else?
- What are you learning? What else?
- What is your plan moving forward?
- Who can provide support for you?
- How can I help you?

Jesus was a master at asking good questions. In the Gospels, he asked 307 questions and chose not to answer to 187 of them. To his disciples, he asked, "*Who do you say I am?*" (Matt 16:15). To a blind man, he asked, "*What do you want me to do for you?*" (Matt 20:32). After calming a storm, he asked his disciples, "*Where is your faith?*" (Luke 8:25). These engaging questions, caused his hearers to think deeply, and prepared their hearts for teaching moments. Though not all of Jesus's questions would be coaching questions, through them we see the value of asking powerful questions to draw a person out.

Listening and asking questions are crucial to coaching. That means that as a coach you will not do much talking. As a rule, the client or disciple speaks about 80 percent of the time. When the coach speaks, it's in the form of questions and affirmations (e.g., *Wow, you were courageous! You love a challenge!*). The coach practices active listening by summarizing or reflecting back what the client has said and by making summary statements. It takes robust self-management to only speak 20 percent of the time. As you interact with your family or work colleagues this week, what percentage of the time are you speaking?

One secret to asking good questions and being an effective coach is curiosity. As we are interested in the client's thoughts and feelings—not for our sake but for theirs—they will also become curious about their own lives and areas of needed growth. Curiosity opens doors for further exploration.

In an environment of listening and asking good questions, a good coach will create a safe space for exploration and discovery. In this space, the client develops trust and is free to explore anything without fear of judgment or criticism.

Coaching to Close the Gap

The gap is the space between where a person is currently and where they want to be. We coach to close the gap. The gap may be a situation in which a person feels stuck. Spiritually, they may feel disconnected from God. Relationally, they may be having a conflict with someone. Physically, they may lack energy or desire to lose weight. As a coach listens well and asks good questions, they will coach to the gap in their client's life.

Conclusion

I've been so encouraged to see how many church leaders in Central Europe, Russia, and Central Asia are applying this new focus of transparent relationships with a coach approach to discipleship. While I opened with some stories about leadership development challenges, let me close with some better stories of church planters and movement leaders in the region who have been helped through this approach.

- For more than fifteen years, a parachurch ministry in Albania has required each staff member to choose a local mentor who will help them to make a personal development plan for the year and meet once a month to evaluate progress. The organization provides ongoing training for the mentors and also encourages everyone to also have an outside mentor to assist with their own spiritual maturity and leadership development. Staff members can also request a "360 feedback" which helps with blind spots and exposes areas of growth.
- A church-planting movement in Belarus has committed to providing mentoring cohorts for every pastor through small group meetings and one-to-one meetings with the facilitator. They have also put together a coaching network for pastors' wives and women in ministry. This strategy builds community and transparency among the leaders.
- A seminary in Ukraine provides training in practical leadership skills as well as theological education. They put the students in learning groups. During the last year, they have connected the students with existing pastors who will mentor them as they plant a new church. The mentors and young pastors return regularly to the seminary for ongoing training and mentoring.

- A parachurch church-planting organization provides training cohorts for movements with multiple churches. Every other week they host webinar teaching. During the off week, a coach meets with the teams individually, to apply what is learned.
- A church-planting movement in Romania hosts an annual pastors and wives retreat where the focus is on marriage and not ministry. Couples enjoy a weekend away from their kids and churches while receiving training for marriage. They also have the option to meet with a Christian therapist.

Bibliography

Amos, Terri. *Women in Ministry Leadership Seminar*. Belarus. May, 2022.

Schindler, Dietrich. "Lessons in Church Planting in Western Europe." Presentation at Columbia International University. November 3, 2022.

Webb, Keith. *The Coach Model for Christian Leaders: Powerful Leadership Skills for Solving Problems, Reaching Goals, and Developing Others*. New York: Morgan James, 2019.

Further Reading

Collins, Gary. *Christian Coaching: Helping Others Turn Potential into Reality*. 2nd ed. Colorado Springs: NavPress, 2009.

Part Four

Mission in Deed

As Christians, we preach the word of God which proclaims the love of God, and we seek to imitate our loving God by loving others as well (Mark 12:28–31; Matt 22:36–40; Luke 10:27 ESV). Jesus modeled what true love looks like by taking sacrificial action on behalf of humanity, and we are exhorted to follow his example:

> By this we know love, that he laid down his life for us, and we ought to lay down our lives for the brothers. But if anyone has the world's goods and sees his brother in need, yet closes his heart against him, how does God's love abide in him? Little children, let us not love in word or talk but in deed and in truth. (1 John 3:16–18 ESV)

Faith that is truly faith is never alone—it is accompanied by deeds of compassion that flow from the deep well of divine love that has taken up residence in the hearts of those who believe. In this section, missional practitioners working in business, medical, and non-profit sectors share ways that they and their teams have been involved in practically loving the communities around them to demonstrate God's care for whole humans living vulnerably in an often precarious world.

Chapter 12

Mission as Transformation

Five Critical Elements

Bekele Shanko

As we look to the future of global Christian mission, I firmly believe it will be driven by transformation: lives that have been changed by the power of the gospel of Jesus Christ. I think of myself, coming from an impoverished, hopeless situation in rural Ethiopia. Yet, God redeemed me and raised me up to be a global leader. In this chapter, I explore five elements that I believe are critical to the future of mission: experiencing personal transformation, practicing intentional collaboration, leveraging the power of technology, ministering to the whole person, and partnering with Global South and Global North churches.

Experiencing Personal Transformation

Over seven hundred years before Christ was born, the prophet Isaiah announced, "The people walking in darkness have seen a great light; on those living in the land of deep darkness a light has dawned" (Isa 9:2 NIV). This news has always inspired me. The prophecy was fulfilled centuries later when Jesus said, "I am the light of the world" (John 8:12 NIV). It will be completely fulfilled at the end of time when we arrive at a glorious place with no darkness, distress, or death.

But the news has a deeper meaning in my life. Before Christ came into my life, my family, and my people, I was like the people who lived "in the area of Zebulun and Naphtali … people living in darkness … in the land of the shadow of death" (Matt 4:13–16 NIV).

Let me take you on a quick journey to a remote village in south-central Ethiopia—the village in which I was born. It is a village with no electricity, no tap water, no evangelical church, no school, and no health service. The village was materially and spiritually poor.

My father served a powerful witch doctor who lived on a mountaintop who also happened to be our relative. He had spiritual power and was able to bring rain, stop rain, and instruct people on issues of life and relationships, crisis and conflicts, and desires and demands. But whenever he was unhappy with people, he cursed them. People died instantly, and the harvest dried up.

Because of his relationship with the witch doctor, my father had similar, but lesser, power and was known as "a man with a black tongue"—meaning his curses had consequences on people and their possessions. At the same time, the witch doctor had given my father too many instructions that were impossible to fulfill. For example, near our thatched-roof hut stood an old coffee tree dedicated to offering sacrifices to evil spirits. My father was required to wake up early every morning and spend several hours smoking and drinking *araki* (an Ethiopian hard liquor). He also had to offer the first portion of every meal to the spirits by placing it under the coffee tree. We were not allowed to eat until the food under the tree was gone. If the food was still there after an hour or so, it meant the spirits were unhappy and my father needed to offer an animal sacrifice. Whenever my father missed a step or did something wrong, a curse would fall on our family, and an otherwise healthy child would immediately die.

My father had three wives, whom he would beat almost daily (often due to the hours of drinking *araki*). Each of these wives had four children die because of these curses—twelve of my eighteen siblings died this way. When I was born, my parents did not give me a name. "Why should we name a child who will probably die?" But when I reached the age of four, they said, "Unusually our child is growing up. Let's give him a name." And they named me Bekele, which in Amharic means, "the seed is germinating, he is sprouting, there is life."

When I was five years old, the witch doctor said to my father, "I see that your son is growing. I want you to train him so that when he grows up, he will serve me." My father made the commitment, and I started following him. We were living a hopeless life, in deep darkness, and in a shadow of death. But one day, the light of the world and the merciful God sent two angels to visit my father in his bed. The two angels sat in front of him and told him about the true God. They explained that God is the one who created the heavens and the earth and everything in them, including my father. After they taught him about God for several hours, the angels said, "We are going to show you what heaven is like and what hell is like."

I cannot explain to you how it happened, but the angels took my father to heaven and showed him what heaven and hell are like. Whenever my father tries to describe his experiences, he gets emotional: "It's so beautiful!

The streets are gold!" he says. The angels also took my father to the gates of hell where he saw people in darkness and screaming, "Please save us!"

After that visit, one of the angels said to my father, "I have shown you two different places, where do you want to be?" My father said, "Please, please, I want to be in heaven!" "Good choice," said the angel. "I will send two men who will tell you how you can get into heaven." For many years, I wondered why the angels did not tell my father how he could get into heaven. But as I grew older, I realized that this glorious mission of introducing people to Jesus is not given to the angels, but to men and women who follow the Lord.

Two days later, on a Friday night, an angel appeared to two men in another village who had only recently become Christians. They were told to visit a man called Shanko (my father) and tell him that the only way he could get into heaven is if he denied demons and believed in Jesus Christ, the Son of God who came to die for the sins of the world. So those two men came to our house at night and said, "We have good news for this family." Four of us were there—my father, my mother, my older sister, and myself.

I remember the scene vividly. As a five-year-old child, I was sitting with my older sister on the floor while my parents sat on chairs. The two men stood in front of us and told my father about Jesus. They said, "If you believe in Jesus, you will stop beating your wives, you will stop drinking, you will stop smoking, and you will also stop serving the witch doctor."

After hearing those words, I stood up, walked over to the two men, and asked, "Really? If my father accepts Jesus, he will stop beating my mom?" They said yes. I didn't know what accepting Jesus meant, but I said if my dad would stop beating my mom, then *I* would accept Jesus. I was the first person in our family to come to Jesus mainly because I wanted dignity for my mother and peace in our family. That night my father, mother, older sister, and myself accepted Jesus, and the gospel of Jesus began to transform our lives.

Two days after we accepted Jesus, another miracle happened in our home. My father had never been to school and was unable to read or write. That day, as he was walking with his cows alongside a river, he found a Holy Bible lying on the ground. We don't know where the Bible came from because at that time we didn't have missionaries in our area. My father picked up the book and opened the pages but didn't know what it was. Suddenly he heard a voice saying, "This is my word." He looked around to see who was speaking to him, but no one was there.

And as he started wondering, "Whose voice was that? What book is this?" Something in his heart said, "Go and sit down under the shade of a tree." He sat down, opened the book, and said, "God, was that your voice? Is this your book? I cannot read it. Can you help me to read it? If you help me to read it, I promise to teach others my whole life."

Right there he began reading the Bible. He came home and said, "I want the whole village to come to my place. I have something important to tell them." Because he had power from the spirits, people feared him and did everything he said. The whole village of a few hundred people filled our compound. My father stood up, opened the Bible, and began to read. He asked people to deny evil spirits and believe in Jesus. That night, the whole village came to Jesus, launching a spiritual revival that swept across our entire tribe and beyond.

For the next thirty-seven years, until he breathed his last at eighty-four, the only book my father could read was the Bible. Once I gave him a Bible and another book in the same Amharic script and asked him to read. He could read the Bible fluently but could not make out a single letter in the other book. "What is wrong with you, my father? Why can't you read the other book?" I asked. "Whenever I open the holy book," he explained, "a bright light shines over my head, and I can see and understand everything. But when I open the other book, it is dark."

God gave my father a supernatural ability to read and teach the Bible and proclaim the good news. A few years ago, the Ethiopian missiologist, Desta Langena, did a survey on our tribe and observed that nearly 94 percent of the 1.6 million people had become evangelical Christians.[1] The mountain where the witch doctor used to live has become a prayer mountain, and the witch doctor has also become a believer.

Every year, between 50,000 and 150,000 people climb the mountain and pray for the whole world, asking God to transform every community as he has transformed ours. This prayer service has taken place every January 19 for the last twenty-five years. Langena's ministry (Ambaricho International Prayer and Mission Movement) is now building a 230-foot-tall cross on the top of the mountain as a testimony to the transforming power of the gospel.[2]

Because of the gospel, our community was also blessed with educational opportunities. I completed high school when I was sixteen years old and graduated from college at nineteen. Due to our abject poverty, I did not get my first pair of shoes until I was thirteen. My parents did not buy them.

---

[1] Langana, *Prayer Movement*, 155.
[2] See further AIPM, "Home."

I actually bought them with my earnings from a primary school I started for children when I was thirteen.

After graduating from Addis Ababa University, I worked with the Ethiopian government for about five years. I worked as head of information management for the national HIV/AIDS Control Program, in partnership with the World Health Organization in Switzerland and the Centers for Disease Control in the USA.

During that time, the Lord called me to full-time missionary service with Campus Crusade for Christ (Cru) where my wife and I have now served for almost three decades. I served as a national director for the ministry in Ethiopia, regional leader for southern and eastern Africa, and global vice president since 2010.

Because of the transforming power of the gospel of Jesus in my life, I am passionately committed to reaching every person in the world with the gospel of Jesus. A transformed person not only has a powerful testimony but *is* a powerful testimony. A transformed person is visible like a light. Therefore, to be effective in the future global mission, we need to experience personal transformation that affects our families, communities, and even nations.

Practicing Intentional Collaboration

The future of global mission must also be about collaboration. No one person, organization, or denomination can fulfill God's global mission alone. It will take all of us who love Jesus and agree that God's kingdom is bigger than any one organization. Mission leaders must be willing to collaborate, humbly learning from one another and generously sharing resources and expertise.

Collaborative leaders cannot say, "Our way is better," or "We have figured it all out." Rather, they must speak the language of "let us." When Nehemiah mobilized the Israelites to rebuild the broken walls of Jerusalem, he said, "Let us rise up and build" (Neh 2:18 ESV). "Let us," expresses humility, selflessness, generosity, and commitment to focus on what is common, what is important, and what is the priority.

When I was leading the national ministry of Cru in Ethiopia, God put in my heart a vision to reach the capital city in fifty-two days—just as Nehemiah completed the rebuilding of the walls of Jerusalem. About three million people lived in the city at the time. Some people did not believe that it would be possible to mobilize the whole body of Christ and reach the whole city in fifty-two days. However, because of intentional collaboration, strategic mobilization of people and resources, division of responsibilities (like what we see in Nehemiah chapter 3), bold leadership and witness, and the favor of God, the project was successfully implemented. Though the evangelical Christian population at the time was only about 3 percent of the city's population, and the church had just come through seventeen years of severe communist persecution, we experienced amazing unity and exemplary collaboration. It was one of the most impactful evangelistic outreaches in the country, with forty-nine thousand people making professions of faith.

Collaboration involves multiple organizations or even multiple countries working together. They can bring their unique gifts, tools, strategies, and experiences, and work together to seize common opportunities, solve common problems, and focus on common priorities. Working together, maximizes resources, minimizes competition and duplication, and strengthens the unity of the body of Christ.

When I was leading the southern and eastern Africa region of Cru (twenty-three countries with a combined population of about 350 million people), God gave me a vision to reach fifty million people in fifty major cities in fifty days in twenty-three countries. It was one of the most amazing and complex projects I have ever led. We mobilized about twenty-one thousand local churches, trained half a million Christians, raised eight million dollars, established nearly two thousand task forces with ten thousand leaders, and developed 103 different strategies of evangelism. At the end of the fifty days, when we gathered reports from all the cities, we realized that we had exceeded our expectations. We saw 64.5 million people exposed to the gospel, while 1.72 million people made professions of faith, including some living outside of the focus cities.

In 2010, I received a phone call from Steve Douglass, then president of Cru. He said, "God is leading us to begin planting churches, and we would like you to establish and lead a church-planting division." At that time, Cru had not officially done church planting. In Africa, however, we had seen so many people come to faith through showing *The Jesus Film* that we naturally gathered them into new churches. So, we already had some experience with church planting.

After I accepted the role, God expanded my vision for the entire world. At that time, the global population had just reached seven billion people (now eight billion as of November 2022). The seven billion was not just a number, it represented people uniquely made in God's image and dearly loved. The seven billion could be divided into two categories: two billion who self-identified as Christians and five billion who did not.

This division gave us two primary responsibilities: First, the two billion who claimed to be Christians needed to be discipled—living out their Christian faith in word, life, and deed. Some of the two billion Christians had never even been to church, and others did not understand what it means to be a Christian. They needed to be equipped and then involved in fulfilling God's mission.

The second part of the mission was to reach the five billion people still waiting to hear the good news. When I facilitated a planning meeting with my new team back in 2010, we talked about these two primary responsibilities and how we could reach the five billion people with the gospel by mobilizing the two billion Christians. That's when God put another number on my heart—*one*. We could plant one healthy church or missional community for every one thousand people worldwide. These churches would be missional, multiplying, sustainable, and making a kingdom impact like the ones we read about in the book of Acts. If we were to plant such a church for every one thousand people in every village, neighborhood, and high-rise apartment building, every digital space, and relational network, and if these churches were to be evenly distributed throughout the world, then we could effectively engage the five billion people with the gospel.

So, with that vision, my family and I moved to the USA and helped launch a church-planting movement for Cru. Now, twelve years later, we have more than twenty-six hundred Cru staff members leading church-planting movements in over 150 countries, and we have seen more than 230,000 churches and missional communities started. The future of global mission is to help Christians to be disciples of Jesus and to mobilize them to take the message of God's love to every person.

Since no single organization can reach five billion people alone, in 2011, the Lord led me to start what we call GACX (a Global Alliance for Church Multiplication).[3] Inspired by Jesus's prayers in John 17 ("that all of them may be one"), I invited leaders from five different organizations to pray together and explore the possibilities of working together. I felt we could inspire, challenge, and support one another, and become a global learning community of church planting movements. We agreed to collaborate and invite other like-minded leaders to join the learning community.

Today, GACX includes over 110 global ministries working together in humility and generosity—sharing resources, tools, and strategies, and

---

3 See further GACX, "Home."

making God's kingdom our priority. At our annual Global Forum, we like to say, "Check your logo at the door," as a reminder that the mission is not about us or our organizations. Rather, it's about the kingdom of God. Since we started collaborating twelve years ago, we have seen about 2.4 million churches and missional communities planted through GACX members. One of our essential practices is the multiplication of disciples, leaders, and churches.

We are continually learning and improving the processes of disciples making disciples, leaders mentoring leaders, and churches planting churches. We insist that a person who is being discipled must be discipling someone else, and a newly planted church should be mobilizing new believers for ministry and raising up new leaders for church multiplication from the very start. As iron sharpens iron, we inspire and learn from one another, improve our tools and strategies, and increase our collective impact. The future of global mission depends on our attitudes and abilities to collaborate with one another.

Leveraging Technology

I believe the future of global mission also lies in our ability to harness technology and to develop digital strategies for mission. What does it mean to share the gospel digitally? What does it mean to plant and multiply healthy churches digitally? What would it look like to make disciples and mentor leaders in a digital space?

The most capable people to help the church navigate the world of technology are the young people. Therefore, it is necessary to build effective partnerships between younger generations and senior leaders in the church. Senior leaders must be both wise enough to empower younger leaders and humble enough to learn from them. At the same time, younger leaders must respect the senior leaders and receive wisdom and mentorship from them. Such intergenerational partnership is not only critical for church health, but is also necessary for the church to be effective and relevant in proclaiming the unchanging message of the gospel in a changing world.

The COVID-19 global pandemic forced the church to learn how to minister to people virtually. Though the technology was available for the church before the pandemic, it was not widely used for ministry. For several weeks at the start of the pandemic, the church panicked because it was not prepared to minister while the doors were shut. Many church leaders realized that they did not have enough people to lead small groups or facilitate virtual church ministries. But after the panic settled and people began to adjust, many churches and leaders began posting live or pre-recorded messages on television, social media, or via Zoom, and distributed podcasts and evangelistic messages digitally. Christian musicians posted live concerts and led worship on Facebook and other platforms.

The pandemic forced the church to recognize and embrace the priesthood of all believers—that every believer can be involved in fulfilling God's mission. Preparing as many leaders as possible to lead and multiply small groups and building the necessary capacity to use technology are crucial for the future of the church. While maintaining the integrity of the word of God and the message of the gospel, believers, and especially ministry leaders, should be encouraged to develop innovative ways of proclaiming the good news, organizing church services, making disciples, and training leaders. Indeed, during the global lockdown, we witnessed the development of many creative ways of doing ministry, including drive-in churches, sending evangelistic video clips and feature films to friends and families, and holding local and international conferences virtually.

Technology enables us to reach places and peoples that we would never be able to reach otherwise. Using technology is also cost-effective. However, to effectively use digital strategies to reach audiences near and far, the church must develop more leaders and be open to the idea of multiplying and missional small groups. By the Holy Spirit's power, discipleship movements, churches (even those facing persecution), and relational communities can be created, sustained, and multiplied through the appropriate use of technology.[4]

Ministering to the Whole Person

If mission is about transformation, then we must preach the whole gospel to the whole person, integrating the spiritual and the material aspects of life. The church has often dichotomized these elements. For example, in the Kale Heywet Church, the largest evangelical church denomination in Ethiopia that nurtured my own spiritual development, there are two major departments—spiritual and development (material). And the two departments don't always work together.

Luke's Gospel emphasizes the holistic development of Jesus: "And Jesus grew in wisdom and stature, and in favor with God and man" (Luke 2:52 NIV). That means Jesus grew intellectually (wisdom), physically (stature),

---

4 See further Frost and Hirsch, *Shaping of Things*.

spiritually (favor with God), and socially (favor with man). When the gospel is preached and practiced in its entirety, it addresses all aspects of a person.

In *The Hole in Our Gospel*, Rich Stearns rightly contends that because of shallow discipleship and our tendency to dichotomize things (i.e., faith and works, spiritual and material, life now and life eternal), we have created a hole in our Christian gospel that needs to be repaired. Stearns argues that a gospel that does not embrace the spiritual, physical, and social dimensions of our life is an incomplete gospel. When we preach a gospel that saves souls but neglects compassion and justice for the poor, our gospel has a hole in it because the hallmarks of the whole gospel include compassion, justice, and proclamation of the good news. In a world full of injustices, famine, disease, and abject poverty, if preached and practiced in its entirety, the gospel will transform individuals and communities.[5]

To experience the transforming power of the gospel, every Christian must be willing to embrace and obey the whole gospel and respond to God's expectation for a higher level of Christian discipleship, authentic personal transformation, responsibility, and compassion. In doing so, we become a voice for the voiceless, we serve others with respect and dignity, we integrate faith and works, rise above the comfort of this world, and uphold the values of love, generosity, and self-sacrifice.

Christians must be motivated by their faith *in Christ* to action *for Christ* and act with urgency to transform one person at a time from the power of poverty, injustices, and suffering. The church must demonstrate the good news of God's kingdom here and now, passionately demonstrating tangible love toward the needy and vulnerable, integrating the great commandment (loving God, loving neighbor) with the Great Commission (making disciples of all nations), and promoting charity, equity, and mercy. When we do so, the world hears and sees the Christian message.

Therefore, proclaiming the whole gospel to the whole person is one of the most important ways in which the gospel message remains relevant and compelling. As every person has spiritual, physical, material, emotional, financial, and psychological needs, the gospel must be preached in such a way that it meets all these needs. Jesus not only said, "You are the light of the world," but also, "you are the salt of the earth" (Matt 5:13–16 NIV).

Highlighting the importance of ministering to the whole person, James argues, "What good is it, my brothers and sisters, if someone claims to have faith but has no deeds?" Then, he concludes, "faith without deeds

---

5 Stearns, *Hole in Our Gospel*.

is dead" (Jas 2:14, 26 NIV). Who wants to practice a dead faith? For our global mission to be effective, we must boldly proclaim the gospel in word, life, and deed.

Global South and Global North Partnerships

The future global mission also depends on our ability to recognize the power of people movements around the world and build strategic partnerships between the church in the Global North (North America and Europe) and the Global South (Asia, Africa, Latin America), where the majority of global Christians now live.

In *The New Faces of Christianity*, Philip Jenkins describes the characteristics and practices of Global South Christianity for a northern audience. He discusses the reasons for Christianity's decline in Western countries (i.e., liberalism, scientism, secularism, apathy toward a biblical worldview). On the other hand, he asserts that Christianity is growing in the Global South because Christians resonate with the cultural world of the Bible and believe that Scripture is authentic and has authority. Further, biblical Christianity provides answers for those facing political, cultural, and socio-economic oppression. The gospel offers a sense of power for the powerless, hope for the poor, security for the persecuted, a framework for political engagement, and guidance for daily life in society.[6]

Regarding the implications of the shift of global Christianity, I ask, following Jenkins, "What mechanisms should be in place to ensure that biblical Christianity not only survives in the Global South but also influences the Global North?" I believe the answer is in our ability to identify and mobilize some of the most important and unique resources each region can contribute toward the common goal of fulfilling Christ's mission in the world.

In the past, we sent missionaries to "dark places" in the world. But today, dark places exist everywhere. It is time to mobilize and send workers and other resources from everywhere to everywhere. For example, the Global North has leadership, experience, strategies, and financial resources. On the other hand, the Global South has dynamic Christianity with contagious enthusiasm and boldness for evangelism—an extraordinary workforce. By bringing these two sets of strengths and opportunities together and developing a common global vision, we can accelerate the fulfillment of God's global mission.

---

6 Jenkins, *New Faces of Christianity*.

Today, due to various factors, millions of believers and non-believers from the Global South have migrated to the countries of the Global North. In these northern cities (i.e., New York, Toronto, Paris), the mission laborers and the mission field have moved into the same neighborhood. The Global North church may not be the best one to engage these new people in our cities. However, through strategic partnerships immigrant churches can go beyond reaching their own people and begin reaching other immigrants with the gospel.

Conclusion

As we reflect on the past one hundred years of global mission, we look to the future, longing to be used by God for his glory among all peoples. I especially pray that young people today will take up the mantle and pray: "I am the future of God's mission. By the grace of God, I will do whatever it takes to promote the message for which Jesus came to die. I will do whatever it takes to see spiritual transformation take place so that God might be glorified, and his mission fulfilled." I also pray that God will help his church apply the five elements I've explored in this chapter—that we will proclaim the gospel in word and deed until Jesus comes.

Bibliography

Frost, Michael, and Alan Hirsch. *The Shaping of Things to Come: Innovation and Mission for the 21st Century*. Grand Rapids, MI: Baker, 2013.

"Home." AIPM. Accessed February 10, 2023. https://www.aipmusa.com.

Jenkins, Philip. *The New Faces of Christianity: Believing the Bible in the Global South*. New York: Oxford University Press, 2006.

Langana, Desta. *Prayer Movement* (Amharic language). Addis Ababa: Zak Printers Press, 2005.

Shanko, Bekele. *Never Alone: From Ethiopian Villager to Global Leader*. Orlando: Global Church Movements, 2021.

Shanko, Bekele, and John Becker. "Building Powerful Partnerships." GACX. Accessed February 9, 2023. https://gacx.io/articles/building-powerful-partnerships.

Stearns, Richard. *The Hole in Our Gospel*. Nashville: Thomas Nelson, 2010.

Chapter 13

We Cracked the Code

Lessons Learned in Business as Mission

Brent McHugh

Soli[1] wasn't allowed to work. Before fleeing his home in the Middle East and applying for asylum in a neighboring nation, he had been pursuing a university education. But as an individual with refugee status, he struggled to support himself. After being accepted by the United Nations High Commissioner for Refugees (UNHCR) as having a "well-founded fear of persecution,"[2] Soli came into contact with a Christar church-planting team and heard the gospel for the first time. He came to faith and was discipled by another believer from his home country, yet he was still without a means to earn an income. But participating in an e-commerce Start-Up Academy changed his story. This training program, launched by Christar workers serving among refugees in Europe,[3] was created to assist displaced people in starting their own businesses—a step that can have a multifaceted ripple effect in refugee communities. Because of his background in textiles, Soli gravitated toward the fashion industry, and opening an online clothing store has been transformative. Today, he pastors a small church in Asia Minor and runs an e-commerce business that provides income for himself and his family members who have also been displaced. The business is his way of engaging the local community for Christ.

The Business as Mission (BAM) Global Think Tank encourages us that, from a Christian perspective, business is a call to transformative service for the good of all. When we are called to serve God, we are charged with taking part in his ministry of transforming people's lives on various levels—personal, institutional, structural, and spiritual. Christ speaks of this transformation in terms of invasion: "your kingdom come, your will be done, on earth as it is in heaven" (Matt 6:10 ESV). The mystery

---

1 Names have been changed.
2 UNHCR, "What is a refugee?"
3 Lee, "Strangers in the Land."

of the incarnation is one of participation—Jesus living among us and experiencing our situations.

Business as Mission forms a crossroads of integrated engagement and proclamation that aligns perfectly with the practitioner's purpose and calling. It understands that we have a responsibility to serve as salt and light in the world for the sake of proclaiming the gospel. Instead of trying to remove Christians from a world that is full of sin and corruption, we seek to be part of the answer to the first petition of the Lord's Prayer, "may your kingdom come" here in this place.

As Soli's story demonstrates, refugee communities present BAM practitioners with an overflow of opportunities to bring about multilevel transformation. In June 2022, the UNHCR noted that the number of forcibly displaced people worldwide had exceeded 100 million—with no end in sight.[4] Those of us who have heard of the 10/40 window can recognize that the vast majority of displaced persons are coming from and residing in this region.[5]

This was the case for Ali, who was forcibly displaced from a Central Asian country and, like Soli, came to Asia Minor and was recognized there as a refugee. The gospel took hold of Ali while he was still trafficking drugs as a means to support himself financially. As Ali began to mature in his faith, he was convicted to leave his involvement with drugs and came to an e-commerce Start-Up Academy.

In the personal development session, Ali revealed that he had worked as a tailor in his home country. This led to the creation of an e-commerce store for suits and jackets that now provides income for Ali and two of his close friends who traveled the refugee highway with him from their home in Central Asia. But the business side of this endeavor was just the beginning. Ali is one of the best evangelists I have ever met. He has led dozens of his compatriots to faith in Christ, including his two friends from his refugee journey. Ali's entire network has heard his personal testimony, and one of his suppliers relayed warmly that in their business meetings, Ali talks more about Jesus than about his product line.

Factors for Fruitfulness

Several factors have contributed to the fruitfulness of the e-commerce Start-Up Academy as a Business as Mission approach that has resulted in more than three hundred e-commerce companies run by immigrants

---

4 UNHCR, "More than 100 Million."
5 UNHCR, "Refugee Data Finder."

and refugees, and has also led to churches being planted among them. The first is the passion of church planters to see holistic transformation in the lives of the people among whom they have been sent to minister. These workers seek to empower entire people groups with access to marketplace opportunities that were previously blocked to them. This passion gives the church planters opportunities to be enfolded into the lives of least-reached people, to proclaim the gospel, and to equip communities to continue the work of the church.

The second factor is the COVID-19 pandemic which has, according to McKinsey & Company, leapfrogged e-commerce ahead. Amit Mathradas reports: "Ten years of e-commerce adoption was compressed into three months. And not only did the shift to an e-commerce-first mindset happen in countries where online shopping was already widely accepted, but it also happened in cultures where in-person, local, cash-reliant, and daily shopping is the norm.[6]

The third factor has been the increase in digital nomad visa programs, particularly in countries that do not offer missionary visas. Through these programs, cross-cultural workers have growing opportunities for integrated engagement in least-reached communities.

Lastly, many refugees and immigrants who have completed the e-commerce Start-Up Academy have had backgrounds that have served as terrific starting points to use their skills and passions in creating e-commerce companies (such as Soli's experience in textiles and Ali's work as a tailor). A displaced mechanic now sells luxury auto parts online; an outdoorsman deals in the latest in hiking and boating equipment; and a beautician runs an online cosmetics store. They were all capable of being entrepreneurs, but they had never considered running their own companies until they were given access to the right training and tools.

Open Opportunities for Integrated Approaches

The global church understands the bivocational pastor. If you have travelled the world, you may have met an attorney pastoring a megachurch in Latin America, a package courier leading a network of house churches in Asia, or a taxi driver in the Middle East who evangelizes everyone he meets. But through Business as Mission, church planters go beyond this dual approach, seeking integration that provides a pathway to work in least-reached communities around the world.

---

6 Mathradas, "Covid-19 Accelerated E-Commerce."

Indeed, the world is wide open for Business as Mission practitioners. Recently a South Asian country that had formerly granted visas no longer than three months for cross-cultural workers, issued five-year business visas for new church planters. To accentuate this open door, we can simply consider the number of incubators in least-reached countries that offer "soft-landing"[7] agreements for entrepreneurs. These opportunities are increasing annually while the number of countries offering business nomad visas expands almost weekly.[8] One South Asian nation, otherwise closed to Christian workers, has a massive start-up campaign that invites entrepreneurs from everywhere to launch companies within its borders.

Compounding this increased access is the reality that you can be a virtual resident of one country and live and work in another through opportunities such as the E-Residency Program of Estonia. "In 2014, Estonia was the first country in the world that launched its E-Residency Program to fulfill its ambition of creating a borderless digital society for global citizens."[9] In 2022, more than eighty-five thousand businesspeople held Estonian e-residency, including several cutting-edge Business as Mission practitioners, allowing them to work anywhere in the world. The possibilities are endless. In addition to Estonia, Azerbaijan, Liberland, Portugal, Lithuania, Ukraine, South Africa, Georgia, Dubai, Japan, Thailand, Singapore, and Brazil currently offer or will likely soon launch e-resident programs.[10] These new options present a wealth of opportunities for BAM practitioners.

Further, we need to consider how people want to go to the mission field. According to "The Future of Missions,"[11] a new research survey from the Barna Group in partnership with the Southern Baptist International Mission Board, the next generation of Christian workers in North America do not want to be mobilized in traditional ways. Our Bible schools and seminaries provide evidence of this shift through the increase in the nontraditional missionary degree programs they offer. Columbia International University, for example, has a business school on campus that did not exist twenty years ago.

The work of integrating business and church planting is nothing new. The current Business as Mission movement championed by Mats

---

7 Starthubcenters, "What Is Soft Landing?"
8 Valencia, "54 DIGITAL NOMAD VISAs."
9 e-Estonia, "e-Identity."
10 Go Visa Free, "e-Residency Programs"; Xolo, "Ultimate list of e-Residency."
11 Barna, "The Future of Missions."

Tunehag is now more than twenty-five years old. However, the concept of Business as Mission is rooted in those who have gone before us. One of the most successful BAM companies in history was started by Moravians in Suriname in the eighteenth century, and it has continued to produce both material and spiritual fruit. In order to serve as Moravian missionaries, humble potters, carpenters, and tailors departed from their home base in Europe to spread the good news of Jesus Christ while using their talents to make a living. Their labor received favor. Two of these missionaries established a tailoring business and launched the Moravian church's activities in Suriname in the first half of the eighteenth century. The church and the tailoring business evolved into the institutions responsible for transforming entire communities, in Suriname as well as in other nations.[12]

Tools for Today's Practitioners

Other colleagues like Hakan Sandberg have developed world-class processes and tools to take Business as Mission practitioners and others from ideation to company creation and acceleration. One of these processes includes the Start-Up Academy, a three-month course (six hours per week plus fieldwork) that assists developing entrepreneurs in laying a strong foundation for their companies.

Historically, most Business as Mission startups fail because their founders think they already know what the marketplace needs or wants, and that they know how to solve the problems their potential customers and clients face. The Academy bases the products and services it offers on overcoming these presumptions. It involves going into the community to test ideas in the real world. Beyond learning to think like entrepreneurs, Academy participants work to shape their business models, validate their assumptions, and create traction for a product or service fitting for their ministry and country of service.

With our partners in the Business and Innovation Center of Europe, Christar has created a free toolbox for Business as Mission trainers and practitioners. The BIC 4 SME Tool Kit[13] presents resources for idea creation, managing the human aspect of business, understanding legal processes, sustaining and growing a company, and expanding a company internationally, among other beneficial tools.

In a recent workshop on Business as Mission, we used the triple bottom line of profitability, sustainability, and church-plantability as the

---
12 MCF Business Enterprises, "About Us."
13 BIC for SME, "SMEs: The backbone."

foundational principles. While articulating a church-planting strategy, we presented a modified lean canvas that included questions about networks and partnerships, key activities, and channels of the message. Using data from the Joshua Project, we chose the Ansari in South Asia as our focus people group, seeking to motivate participants to see themselves as individuals who would go to this large, least-reached group and plant churches among them. Several of the participants were surprised at the depth of information that was readily available about using their professional skills and interests among these people and that industries like food processing were abundant in their marketplaces.

The presentation showed how Business as Mission practitioners can be enfolded into least-reached communities, share the gospel through business, establish a community on God's Word, equip people for ministry, and invite others to serve. In the case of Soli, whose story was used as a case study, a Business as Mission e-commerce company has given him access to a whole new mission field among his community.

The two most fruitful practices in church planting, according to the Seed to Fruit study,[14] were knowing the language and having a respected name in the community. Soli, who has learned the majority language of his host country well, reported that approaching his community as a businessperson changed the relational dynamic for the good and has given him increased acceptance in his community. His connections with the townspeople are leading to open doors for proclaiming the good news to others.

Conclusion

In conclusion, let me share three final thoughts. First, Start-Up Academies like the one presented here give displaced people and those on the refugee highway access to tools to start their own businesses and access to e-residencies that enable them to receive income. Secondly, Business as Mission facilitators can embed Start-Up Academies in the communities they want to reach. These tools and processes allow them to engage a huge felt need among many unreached peoples. Finally, through e-commerce, Business as Mission practitioners can be deployed and engage in many closed-access countries for the purpose of church planting among them.

---

14 Woodberry, *From Seed to Fruit*.

Bibliography

B., David. "What Is Soft Landing?" *Starthub Centers*, August 4, 2017. https://starthubcenters.com/what-is-soft-landing/.

BAM Global: Business as Mission. "Home." Accessed January 31, 2023. https://bamglobal.org.

Barna. "The Future of Missions." Accessed January 30, 2023. https://shop.barna.com/products/the-future-of-missions.

BIC for SME. "SMEs: The Backbone of EU Economy." Accessed January 30, 2023. https://www.bicforsme.eu/.

e-Estonia. "e-Identity." Accessed January 30, 2023. https://e-estonia.com/solutions/e-identity/e-residency/.

Go Visa Free. "e-Residency Programs Around the World: The Ultimate Guide in 2023." Updated April 11, 2023. Accessed December 27, 2023. https://govisafree.com/e-residency-program-countries.

Lee, Morgan. "Strangers in the Land of Startups." *Christianity Today*, May 23, 2019. https://www.christianitytoday.com/news/2019/may/malaga-refugees-startup-entrepreneurship-tech-hub-spain.html.

Mathradas, Amit. "Covid-19 Accelerated E-Commerce Adoption: What Does It Mean For The Future?" *Forbes*, December 29, 2020. https://www.forbes.com/sites/forbesbusinesscouncil/2021/12/29/covid-19-accelerated-e-commerce-adoption-what-does-it-mean-for-the-future/?sh=37acad80449d.

MCF Business Enterprises. "About Us." Accessed January 30, 2023. https://mcfbe.com/about-mcf/.

UNHCR. "More than 100 Million Now Forcibly Displaced: UNHCR report." June 16, 2022. https://news.un.org/en/story/2022/06/1120542.

UNHCR. "Refugee Data Finder." Accessed January 30, 2023. https://www.unhcr.org/refugee-statistics/download/?url=F8Wzj7.

UNHCR. "What Is a Refugee?" Accessed January 30, 2023. https://www.unhcr.org/what-is-a-refugee.html.

Valencia, Maria. "54 DIGITAL NOMAD VISAs Offered by Countries in 2023." *Traveling Lifestyle*, Updated March 19, 2023. https://www.travelinglifestyle.net/countries-offering-digital-nomad-visas-and-residency/.

Woodberry, J. Dudley, ed. *From Seed to Fruit: Global Trends, Fruitful Practices, and Emerging Issues among Muslims*. Littleton, CO: William Carey Publishing, 2021.

Xolo (blog). "Ultimate List of e-Residency Countries in 2023." Updated January 6, 2023. https://blog.xolo.io/ultimate-list-of-e-residency-countries.

Chapter 14

Long-Term Medical Mission in the Middle East

Dae-Young Lee

Shalom and Medical Mission

Shalom is the ultimate reality that God desires for all of humanity and his creation. From the original Hebrew, "shalom" can be simply translated as "peace," but it has a much deeper biblical concept than only the absence of hostility and strife. Amid brokenness caused by humanitarian crises in the Middle East, people long to experience shalom. Because of creation's fallen state, no one will experience shalom without God's divine intervention. Jesus has fulfilled his task to open the door to shalom through a restored relationship with God.

Shalom can be manifested in the practice of medicine through caring for patients individually and restoring their communities. While pain marks the Middle East, it does not reduce the people's warmth and kindness and their desperation for the gospel. In the face of suffering, people can experience God's shalom, healing, and transformation—what Jesus demonstrated in his earthly ministry. Just as Jesus encountered marginalized people with compassion, believers can express that same compassion today through faithful medical mission to those despairing from deadly violence. The gospel of peace shows the only way to transform people and their societies. Biblical shalom will transform social structures that perpetuate spiritual blindness and oppression through compassionate Christian medical mission.

Medical Mission Today

War, economic decline, natural disasters, and the COVID-19 pandemic have directly affected many households around the world. The growing global church is pursuing mission while global ideologies antagonistic to mission are also spreading. Massive movements of people and rapid urbanization are resulting in significant cultural and social changes, and the gap between the Global North and the Global South is growing.

Despite being persecuted in the Muslim world, the church has been growing in places where it has never been before. Christian medical mission work has a unique role to play in the Christian mission endeavor. Professional medical practice allows for proximity, credibility, and the opportunity to share the gospel of Christ with people in need.

Healing is a central concern of medicine, and the goal of healing is recovery or restoration. Healing is a dynamic process of recovering from a trauma or illness through proper medical practices. Christian medical care should be holistic, revealing the true identity of Christ, and caring for the patient's physical and spiritual needs. An encounter with the person of Christ through Christian medical mission brings new fellowship with Christ which restores God's image in fallen human beings. Additionally, the most spiritually, materially, and socially impoverished people should be prioritized in parts of the world where the good news of Jesus is least known.

Christian medical mission must demonstrate the whole character of God and his mighty acts of redemption through professional medical care. Even though Christian medical missions have provided outstanding care in medically underdeveloped countries for decades, it is not uncommon for well-known Christian mission clinics and hospitals to struggle to maintain their services. The major challenge they face is the lack of financial and human resources, as they are largely dependent on foreign support. Furthermore, Christian medical mission efforts have often ignored or dismissed local healthcare systems because they did not share biblical values. At times, short-term teams have brought medicine into the country and distributed it without the permission of local health authorities. Good intentions should not be used to justify illegal activities on the mission field. Indeed, paternalistic attitudes from Christian medical missionaries have often resulted in dependency and short-sighted approaches have led to negative consequences for the local healthcare system.

Our Journey in Medical Mission in the Middle East

The government hospital in the Middle East where we worked was extremely underdeveloped because of the poor support from the government and the lack of proper management. Although this kind of underdeveloped hospital often requires immediate, emergency humanitarian help, a different approach to establishing a self-sustaining and vibrant healthcare system was needed for a long-term solution. Since inadequate medical and nursing training directly contributes to the high morbidity and mortality rates, training initiatives for the local medical professionals was the most important ministry in this context.

One of the most important goals of medical missions that my wife and I pursued was to encourage local healthcare workers to use their full potential through discovering their own capacity and resources on hand. It may take longer for the local medical professionals to understand new ways of medical practice and values but once they come to accept them as their own practices, they become sustainable. We respectfully invited doctors and nurses there to consider new ways of enhanced medical care. This provided an opportunity for us to work closely with the local health care workers who desired to grow professionally. Many of them became proficient and independent leaders who were able to train the next generation of workers and also other co-workers at different hospitals in the area. Eventually, the local teaching staff was able to lead the training programs independently.

During the third year of our CPR training program, a severely ill patient—the uncle of our hospital director—was brought into our ward at the hospital. He had a heart attack soon after he was admitted. Our code blue team, the first one in this hospital's history, successfully helped the patient recover from his heart attack after performing CPR for thirty minutes. Many people at the hospital, including the hospital director and the leadership, were amazed by his recovery. Because of this event, many of the hospital staff were eager to join the training programs to learn more. Even after our forced departure from the country at the onset of a civil war, the local training staff continued the training programs despite the difficult circumstances. Additionally, the nursing training programs earned a notable reputation among the medical societies in the region and within the local government. The training staff was even invited to teach at other hospitals.

This project strove to establish a model of a compassionate and counter-cultural medical practice with a high standard of ethics and medical professionalism. In addition to improved medical skills, those facilitating this project were confronting the culture of corruption, incompetence, inefficiency, and apathy that was endemic in the local public health care system. Through this medical ministry, Christian doctors and nurses were able to minister holistically to the physical, emotional, and spiritual needs of the local people. The expatriate medical team was actively involved in ministry, praying before and after surgeries and visiting patients and their families.

It is important to find a way to encourage the growth of something that is indigenous in order to produce long-term spiritual fruit. It may take longer to find a sustainable structure for the local healthcare system, but such a structure becomes invaluable and strongly influential once established. Throughout the process of implementing medical missions, local medical professionals should not only be trained in their medical practices but also be challenged with a holistic approach of medicine so that they may be influenced by Christian values. This will help Christian medical missions continue to be influential in their communities in partnership with the local healthcare professionals even after the international mission community withdraws completely. The medical staff at the hospital where we served received honor and praise from the medical communities as well as from patients who were treated, encouraging them to grow with the assistance of the Christian medical mission.

During these medical missions, a vision for Arabs to Arabs was cast in which we empowered and assisted Arab Christian medical professionals to reach out to their own people. We have been encouraged to see long-standing churches in the Middle East share the gospel with Muslims in spite of many challenges and persecution. Christian medical mission teams must search for ways to work with these churches to fulfill the Great Commission by establishing and nurturing new churches. As Arab Christian medical professionals and churches understand the language and culture better than foreigners, they will make medical missions in the region more effective and efficient. Instead of building their own institutions, Christian medical missionaries should recognize the important role that the local churches play. This effort acknowledges their potential with the hope of nurturing the medical ministries to be sustained by the local Christian community. An Egyptian transplant surgeon in the United States was willing to come and help with our medical missions. Fluent in Arabic, he was able to build a very close relationship with the local surgeons and shared the gospel message in culturally relevant ways.

Short-term medical missions are an important part of the Christian mission, but undesirable effects develop when they are not strategically planned. Primary care and distribution of prescribed medication should not be prioritized unless a situation such as a natural disaster requires it. Medicine provided free of charge by short-term medical missions may very well disrupt the local healthcare system and break the local patient-doctor rapport. Short-term medical missions have great potential when they are coordinated with and serve the local healthcare system.

The turmoil caused by civil war in the Middle East led us to a very different type of medical mission work. Refugees from Syria and Iraq were forced to leave their homelands with only what they could carry. They lived in desperate poverty. Relief work combined with medical care for the refugees was initiated to respond to their pain and suffering. This medical project focused on providing medical care, preventing diseases, promoting health, and reducing health inequalities among the refugees. As part of this, Elpis HOME Clinic was established as a stationary clinic to provide primary medical care for refugee patients. This clinic regularly provided health awareness programs. Most of the poverty-prone refugees were deprived of education and therefore had little knowledge about how to maintain good health and to recognize its benefits in daily life. The health awareness program helped refugees to develop a disease-free lifestyle and control chronic illnesses through healthy lifestyle habits and preventing infectious diseases.

In addition to the stationary clinic, mobile clinics served the most impoverished people with the healing message of Christ and primary medical care in the highly populated refugee areas near the Syrian border. While patients waited to see physicians, various health awareness programs were offered by local health educators. Wherever the mobile clinic went, the staff collaborated with local churches that were ministering among refugees in those areas. This collaboration established a long-term healthcare system with local healthcare workers, volunteers, refugee communities, and local churches.

A vital part of this ministry was visiting patients in their homes. Patients who would not come to the clinic for various reasons were taught how to take care of themselves at home but were also encouraged to come to the clinic to receive advanced care. A visiting nurse and her staff provided an informative session on preventive medicine in people's homes where they felt more at ease. Gaining a greater understanding of the family's current living condition allowed the caregivers to develop a more intimate relationship with the families. Since the bond of trust between patient and physician is vital to the medical care process, this medical ministry offered opportunities to improve the quality of life and health of the refugee families.

From the beginning, this project included a counseling program offered through a local Christian psychologist to support families struggling with serious emotional and spiritual issues. Many of the refugees had experienced profound loss and survived devastating events that seriously impacted their emotional development and long-term functionality. Their flight from their home countries was marked by violence and instability as well as long periods without basic necessities such as proper nutrition, housing, and education. The counseling program was only the beginning of understanding the impact of armed conflict, displacement, and resettlement, particularly on the children. This program aimed to help refugee families learn to cope with their emotional and spiritual issues.

Conclusion

A top priority for Christian medical mission should be collaborating with growing local churches for long-term sustainability and a culturally relevant structure. Local churches and organizations should assume leadership soon after the medical ministry is established to pursue proper contextualization and develop long-term sustainability. This practice will also encourage Arab Christian medical professionals to be a part of God's mission and provide the global church with strategic ways of reaching out to the unreached in the Middle East. Christian medical mission should strive to reflect the values that Suzanne Hurst articulates: to be "Community-based, People-centered, People-owned, Participative, Focused on targeting the root cause of the problem, Measurable, and Sustainable."[1]

Christian medical mission has played a momentous role in God's mission by humbly taking a position of lowliness while serving the sick and the marginalized. Through this work, many people have been reached with the gospel and churches have been established. God opens doors in unexpected ways for Christian medical missionaries to meet people living in areas closed to the gospel. At this moment in history, we should humbly reflect what we have done well and what we have done poorly. With a deeper understanding of the current global context, we must continue to pursue a biblical and concrete way of bringing shalom to individuals and communities through holistic care and proclamation of the gospel.

Bibliography

Hurst, Suzanne. "Best Practices in Compassionate Mission." In *For the Love of God: Principles and Practices of Compassion in Missions*. Edited by Jerry M. Ireland. Eugene, OR: Wipf and Stock, 2017.

---

1 Hurst, "Best Practices."

Further Reading

Bendor-Samuel, Paul. "Holistic Ministry in an Islamic Context: Initial Reflections." In *Doing Mission in the Arab World*. Edited by John Stringer, 1–18. Groningen, The Netherlands: Grassroots Mission Publications, 2008.

Corbett, Steve, and Brian Fikkert. *When Helping Hurts: How to Alleviate Poverty without Hurting the Poor and Yourself*. Chicago: Moody, 2012.

DeYoung, Kevin, and Greg D. Gilbert. *What Is the Mission of the Church? Making Sense of Social Justice, Shalom, and the Great Commission*. Wheaton, IL: Crossway, 2011.

Lee, Dae-Young. *Shalom: God's Ultimate Purpose for the World: Modern Medical Mission in the Islamic Context*. Eugene, OR: Wipf & Stock, 2021.

Miller, Darrow L. *Discipling Nations: The Power of Truth to Transform Cultures*. Seattle: YWAM Publishing, 2001.

Chapter 15

Best Practices in Short-Term Medical Mission

Jill McElheny

The Call

Working in international missions requires a different set of skills than are needed in an American setting. It takes a different level of compassion and stamina to work in difficult conditions. Christian medical professionals called to short-term medical mission work must be able to discern if they are called to serve in this way. In Luke 5:27, Jesus said to Levi, "Follow me." He does not say, "Follow me *if*" or "Follow me *when*." His simple instructions are to get up and go. I first discovered this verse after receiving my first disaster deployment call in 2010. I did not have the details arranged for my emergency department shifts to be covered, for my children to be picked up from school, or for any of my other responsibilities. Responding to the disaster required me literally to follow him, and to prayerfully trust in his divine foresight as I was called to serve for an undetermined length of time in disaster-stricken Haiti.

After working for a period of time in the aftermath of that disaster, it became apparent to me that God knew exactly the team he was putting together for this mission. Our team was a perfect mix of so many different skills—orthopedic surgeons, anesthesiologists, plastic surgeons, trauma nurses, and me. I was an older, more seasoned trauma nurse practitioner who could prioritize quickly and help mentor the younger team members. When you think that God can't use you, you have to trust that he knows exactly what he is doing when he calls you.

A team member reminded me that God does not call us to run the race that we set for ourselves. I always knew I wanted to work in medical missions, but I had never really planned on going to work in disasters. Hebrews 12:1 tells us to "Run … the race set before us." To be able to hear the call, you have to be listening. Another disaster team member emphasizes the importance of always abiding in Christ (John 15:4) to be able to discern the call.

Biblical Reflections

While working as a nurse, it is important to remain grounded in Scripture. The challenges involved with serving others require that we stay rooted in our faith. I would like to share some Scriptures that I have used for support.

Luke 10:9 (ESV)

Sending his disciples on mission, Jesus said, "Heal the sick … and tell them, 'The kingdom of God has come near to you.'" Whether we're serving in our hometown or in another culture, people have deeply held beliefs about sickness and health. No matter where Christian medical professionals are serving, this verse is central to the way we care for patients. Though we may not always be able to completely heal the sick in the way most think of healing, we can provide them hope in the name of Jesus. Patients often ask, "Why do you do this work?" or "How do you work in such hard conditions?" These questions present a great opening to share with patients that we do this work to serve as the hands and feet of Jesus Christ.

2 Corinthians 1:3–5, 7 (ESV)

The Apostle Paul wrote:

> Blessed be the God and Father of our Lord Jesus Christ, the Father of mercies and the God of all comfort, who comforts us in all our affliction, so that we may be able to comfort those in any affliction with the comfort with which we ourselves are comforted by God. For as we share abundantly in Christ's sufferings, so through Christ we share abundantly in comfort too … Our hope for you is unshaken, for we know that as you share in our sufferings, you will also share in our comfort.

While serving during a short-term mission, I was caring for an older gentleman who had suffered many broken bones during an earthquake. I learned he had lost his home and his wife, and that his son was with him in the hospital where I was working. One night, the man and his son watched me for hours working in the hospital, and then they called me over to the bedside. The son said, "My father wants to pray for you." I replied, "For me? You're the ones who need prayer! You've lost everything." The older man replied, "I'm sure you have a nice home and a nice family. You've left all of that to come work here. You say you are doing that to serve your God, so your God must be real." Providing comfort to those who are suffering also shows them the hope of Jesus Christ.

Romans 8:18 (ESV)

Paul also wrote, "For I consider that the sufferings of this present time are not worth comparing with the glory that is to be revealed to us." Medical professionals see so much suffering and so many things that just don't make sense. I worked in hospice for a few years, where all of my patients were dying. We can learn a lot from people who are dying. It was actually one of my patients who shared Romans 8:18 with me. He told me that the suffering he was having in this world was no match for the glory he was about to receive.

Another one of my hospice patients was a little old lady. When I asked her if she wanted CPR if her heart stopped, she replied, "Don't you stop me! I have a mansion waiting for me in heaven!" She was confident of the glory she was about to receive. She died that night, peacefully.

Guiding Values

Building on this sense of calling and these foundational Scriptures, what guiding values and principles ought to shape our work in short-term medical mission? I suggest five here.

Teamwork

Teamwork is essential to successful care when working in international short-term mission. All team members must be flexible in order to perform many different roles and to adapt to rapidly changing conditions. Teamwork is critical when working in difficult conditions and dealing with an already vulnerable population. One colleague put it this way:

> Often on the field, we all seem to have a clear picture of what we are battling outside—whether Ebola or ISIS. There are no questions about the enemy in disaster, and therefore we run toward it. This is where the true enemy can lay seeds of bitterness, resentment, or jealousy in our hearts, as he tries to tear us down from within. Therefore, not only exhibiting Christ's love to others, but being centered in his person, and walking in his Spirit are critical to successful teamwork.[1]

The need for teamwork becomes evident from the moment the team arrives on site. All team members arrive with different levels of experience

---
1 Personal communication, 2018.

and different skill sets, and all come from different clinical settings. The team members usually don't know each other, and they must quickly coordinate the functions of the team. God's hand is always evident in the assembly of the team. The skills of each member seem divinely coordinated to perform the work to function as the hands and feet of Christ. Again, my colleague remarks: "We need all experiences and backgrounds, just as we need the different members of the body."[2]

All members of a medical team serving in short-term medical missions must be willing to perform a variety of functions while working in unfamiliar settings. Although a nurse may have skills and experience in one area, he or she may be required to care for patients in a completely different clinical area during a disaster. Similarly, surgeons who are used to working in technologically sophisticated operating suites may be required to perform primary care duties or even basic patient care duties. A nurse who has spent the first several days of deployment working as a triage nurse may then be asked to work in a medical-surgical ward or another area of the field hospital due to changes in patient flow.

Cultural Care

While working internationally, or sometimes even in one's own community, medical professionals encounter cultures with different beliefs, customs, and practices. An awareness of these differences is essential to provide the best care in cross-cultural service.

Madeline Leininger's theory of culture care diversity and universality was developed to establish a substantive knowledge base to guide nurses in the discovery and use of transcultural nursing practices. Leininger believed that differences in culture greatly affect the way that nurses are able to provide adequate care to a patient with diverse beliefs and customs that differed from the nurses' home cultures. As nurses care for patients from diverse backgrounds, they will encounter fear and even resistance to health personnel, which can lead to misunderstandings, frustration, and even misdiagnoses.[3]

---

2 Personal communication, 2018.

3 See further Leininger, "Leininger's Theory of Nursing," 152–60; and Smith and Parker, *Nursing Theories*.

Leininger identified three nursing concepts that achieve culturally congruent care for patients: cultural preservation or maintenance, cultural care accommodation or negotiation, and cultural care re-patterning or restructuring. Her culture care theory defines nursing as a profession that focuses on care to support patients in a culturally sensitive way. This theory closely aligns with the challenges encountered by all medical professionals in the field while caring for patients in international settings.[4]

Sustainable Relief

It is important for those serving in short-term medical missions to provide patients with sustainable relief. Sustainable relief includes being sensitive to the aftermath of relief efforts. Teams should never leave a country with unfinished tasks. Although we may have only scheduled a one- or two-week trip, we want to ensure that there is appropriate follow-up care, whether that care is physical, emotional, or spiritual.

It is difficult for victims to continue to recover following a disaster if the care provided is only immediate care and does not support full recovery. Examples of sustainable relief may include both medical care and other types of support. Patients who have received surgery or other types of care, such as sutures, casting, or medical device placement, may require follow-up care to ensure they have optimal chances of recovery. Victims of disaster who have lost their homes, jobs, and food supply may require construction, economic, and agricultural support to aid in their overall recovery.

Follow-Up Care

Medical care provided to victims during the days, weeks, and months following a disaster is essential. Diseases and epidemics can result in populations affected by disaster and subsequent displacement. Examples of good follow-up care may include patient education, continuation of medical treatments started, or education for national medical staff members. Follow-up clinics can provide much-needed medical support for patients requiring post-surgical care. Education and prophylaxis to prevent the spread of disease can help thwart the onset of epidemics in nations whose infrastructure is damaged by a disaster. The cholera epidemic following the Haiti earthquake is an example of how education could have prevented the rapid spread of a deadly disease.

---

4 Petprin, "Leininger's Culture Care Theory."

Debriefing

Medical professionals who work in disaster settings require debriefing to process their experiences. A debriefing session with a group of team members seeks to prevent long-term problems by encouraging those who have been exposed to stressful events to share their experiences. Group debriefing should be a safe place for all members to share without criticism or judgment, and all shared information should remain confidential. Positive aspects of the ministry should be discussed along with difficult topics.[5]

The Multiple Stressor Debriefing (MSD) model was developed for debriefing team members at the end of a disaster relief response. It includes four phases:

1. Disclosure of Events: The purpose, rules, and phases of the session should be outlined. Each member shares one or two distressing events.
2. Feelings and Reaction: Discussion of thoughts and feelings.
3. Discussion of coping strategies.
4. Termination: Discussion of the transition back to home life.

Although team members may be tempted to avoid debriefing after a disaster response or may discount the process, it is essential for the team to process events with others who have experienced similar situations and events during a disaster response. It is sometimes difficult to identify positive aspects of a disaster response, and nurses have often struggled to understand the purpose of mass casualty. Here, it is good to reflect on a Scripture like Isaiah 55:8, "For my thoughts are not your thoughts, neither are your ways my ways, declares the LORD."

Conclusion

Jesus said, "The harvest is plentiful, but the laborers are few" (Matt 9:37). Given the number of natural disasters around the world and the significant human suffering accompanying them, this verse certainly applies to the work of medical ministry. We must be rooted and grounded in Scripture. We must work as teams to be sensitive to culture, provide sustainable care and follow-up, and debrief our deployments of service. As Christian medical professionals, we want to respond to God's call to use our skills and training to relieve suffering.

---

5 For more information on debriefing, see Samaritan's Purse, *Disaster Assistance Response Team*.

Bibliography

Leininger, M. M. "Leininger's Theory of Nursing: Cultural Care Diversity and Universality." *Nursing Science Quarterly* 1, no. 4 (1988): 152–60.

Petrprin, A. "Leininger's Culture Care Theory." *Nursing Theory*. Accessed January 30, 2023. http://www.nursing-theory.org/theories-and-models/leininger-culture-care-theory.php.

Samaritan's Purse. *Disaster Assistance Response Team (DART) Manual*. Boone, NC: Samaritan's Purse, 2015.

Smith, M. C., and M. E. Parker. *Nursing Theories and Nursing Practice*. Philadelphia: F.A. Davis, 2015.

Further Reading

Mauk, Kristen L., and Mary E. Hobus. *Nursing as Ministry*. Burlington, MA: Jones and Bartlett, 2021.

Chapter 16

Best Practices for Refugee Ministry in the Middle East

Jairo de Oliveira

It was still dark when Abdu Ali and his two younger brothers, Youssef and Mohammad, fled Raqqa, Syria's former ISIS capital. They intended to reach the Jordanian territory and seek refuge at Zaatari refugee camp. Two days later, after driving more than 360 miles south and crossing the border, the three Syrian boys arrived at the world's second-largest refugee camp, home to over one hundred thousand Syrian refugees. Abdu Ali and his brothers left behind their parents and five other siblings in Raqqa. Unfortunately, Abdu Ali's parents did not have enough funds to pay for all the costs for the entire family to get to Zaatari. Therefore, they sent only three of their children to Jordan.

Fifteen months after his arrival in Jordan, Abdu Ali attended a youth camp organized by local Christians. For the first time in his life, the seventeen-year-old Syrian boy heard the gospel message in his mother tongue. The Lord opened the door of faith to Abdu Ali, and he eagerly accepted the opportunity to experience the miracle of new birth. "I thank God for the war in Syria," Abdu Ali said on the day of his baptism. "Although I am deeply sorry for the devastation it has caused, without the war that forced me to flee my country, I would not have had the opportunity to receive the good news."

An Unprecedented Crisis

We are living in a historic era of global migration. Christopher Wright draws attention to this issue with an intriguing remark: "There are more migrants in the world today than probably at any time in human history."[1] Refugees, asylum seekers, and Internally Displaced People (IDP) are among the most affected by the current global migration movement. According to the United Nations High Commissioner for Refugees (UNHCR) statistics, this group makes up over 100 million people worldwide.[2]

---

1 Wright, *Scattered and Gathered*, xvii.
2 UNHCR, "Refugee Data Finder."

Clearly, the migration crisis is a humanitarian catastrophe that has shaped generations. Research has proven that the world's population of forcibly displaced people has grown significantly over the last two decades.[3] Unfortunately, the growing conflicts around the world indicate that the current migration crisis will not be easily or quickly resolved. The current global situation suggests that the disastrous circumstances involving millions of refugees are a reality that will continue to impact millions of lives and shape the future of global mission in the coming years and decades.

Real People

When we consider the current state of the migration crisis, we must keep in mind that we are dealing with much more than statistics or numbers. The crisis affects real people: men, women, and children who, like Abdu Ali and his brothers, have been forced to leave their homes and are now moving around the world "harassed and helpless, like sheep without a shepherd" (Matt 9:36 NIV).

The testimony of Abdu Ali affirms that the current migration crisis presents both challenges and opportunities. Therefore, we should be vigilant not to lose our ability to care for those who are on the move, and we should rethink how to fulfill God's mission in our generation. Tira and Jackson assert: "The current trends and realities of migration and diaspora require missiologists and mission practitioners to re-evaluate cherished theories and practices of mission that remain territory-specific and geographically focused."[4]

The Basis for Our Involvement

Migration is a central theme in the Bible. From Genesis to Revelation, we find men and women crossing borders and interacting with people from other cultural contexts as part of their walk with the Lord. Jenny Hwang Yang affirms this by saying, "Scripture is a story of people in exile and on the move, and many of the prominent characters in the Bible had a migration experience which was fundamental to their experience of God."[5]

The Bible teaches that God "loves the foreigner" (Deut 10:18 NIV). Consequently, God commands his people to love the foreigner living

---

3 UNHCR, "Global Trends 2021."

4 Tira and Jackson, "Responding to the Phenomenon," 98.

5 Yang, *Global Diasporas and Mission*, 152.

among them, "And you are to love those who are foreigners" (Deut 10:19 NIV). In several biblical passages, God's people are instructed to treat foreigners well and even to treat foreigners in the same way that they treat their countrymen: "The foreigner residing among you must be treated as your native-born. Love them as yourself, for you were foreigners in Egypt. I am the LORD your God" (Lev 19:34 NIV).

God loves the foreigner because he is impartial towards people and loves every human being without distinction. God taught this aspect of his nature to Peter in a vision in the city of Joppa. Consequently, Peter declared, "I now realize how true it is that God does not show favoritism" (Acts 10:34–35 NIV).

Interestingly, the Scriptures describe all of God's people as "foreigners and exiles" (1 Pet 2:11 NIV) whose "citizenship is in heaven" (Phil 3:20 NIV). This expression is used to illustrate the temporary condition we hold in this life. God's plan is that while we await our heavenly country (Heb 11:16), we should have compassion for those who wander among us and need our powerful manifestations in deeds and words (Luke 24:19 NIV).

God Leads the Story

Even though the migration crisis represents a humanitarian catastrophe, we need to remember that God is ultimately the Lord of history so these movements of people have not taken him by surprise. The Scriptures teach us that God is in control of all mankind's times and locations. By divine power, the Almighty allows people to move around the globe and inhabit the whole earth with the purpose of letting them seek and know him. Luke writes:

> From one man he made all the nations, that they should inhabit the whole earth; and he marked out their appointed times in history and the boundaries of their lands. God did this so that they would seek him and perhaps reach out for him and find him, though he is not far from any one of us. (Acts 17:26, 27)

From a missiological standpoint, the global migration crisis has a strategic component. It has dispersed many cultural groups who were previously isolated from the Christian faith and placed them in contexts where they are much closer to the gospel. Muslim countries with no religious freedom, such as Afghanistan, Somalia, and Sudan, are at the heart of the current migration crisis. People from these countries are now migrating to North America and Europe where religious freedom is regarded as a fundamental right. In the West, they have the freedom to continue practicing Islam while also being exposed to the Christian faith. Consequently, many Afghans, Somalis, and Sudanese are learning about Jesus and becoming his disciples. Therefore, as we examine the scenario of today's refugee reality, it becomes clear that the global migration crisis also represents an opportunity for the church to fulfill the Great Commission given by Jesus in Matthew 28:19: "Therefore go and make disciples of all nations, baptizing them in the name of the Father and of the Son and of the Holy Spirit."

God is conducting world history, even in the most difficult times. The Almighty is working through the church and doing his work amid diaspora movements. The opportunities are immense. Brian Hébert writes: "Missions to the diaspora affords opportunities to reach peoples from closed access countries without the necessary approval from foreign governments. Missions through the diaspora mobilize people who have natural connections to closed access countries."[6]

Ten Best Practices

Given these foundational principles, I would like to present ten best practices for refugee ministry. These practices have served me well in my work with refugees in South Africa, Kenya, Sudan, the United States, and now the Middle East. They have proven to be fruitful, and I am confident that they can be applied to many other contexts because they foster relationship building, address perceived needs of refugees, and provide excellent opportunities for Christian witness.

Teaching the Local Language

Teaching refugees the local language is critical for their adaptation to a new place. Language acquisition has the potential to transform the lives of refugees who are displaced to a new environment where they are unable to communicate with the locals. As we interact with refugees, we can assist them by providing formal or informal language classes. Many churches in the United States have made teaching English as a second language (ESL) a key ministry tool.

Helping with Translation

When refugees cannot communicate in the local language, helping them with translation is also essential. Finding people who speak their language and can serve as translators is incredibly helpful while refugees are still learning the local language. This kind of assistance is required for various daily tasks, such as scheduling appointments, opening a bank account, or reading mail.

---

6 Hébert, "'With' of Diaspora Missiology," loc. 3384.

Tutoring

Given that refugees have been resettled in our community and are unlikely to speak the local language, tutoring will be one of the most important kinds of help they can receive. Refugees rely on tutoring to assist them or their children in overcoming their educational challenges, particularly at the beginning of their resettlement process.

Cultural Orientation

Refugees may come from a culture that is vastly different from that of their new host country. Cultural differences can cause misunderstandings and conflict and have an emotional impact on our refugee friends. Helping them understand the ways of life in their new cultural environment can protect them from much embarrassment and many problems.

Logistical Training

It is critical to assist the foreigner in understanding how to adjust to life in their new environment. Many practical aspects of life can appear strange to a refugee who has recently resettled. When refugees arrive in a foreign country and do not know how to do things that most people do instinctively, they may become disoriented. Helping refugees learn how to do things such as use public transportation, shop for groceries, and schedule doctor's appointments can make a significant difference in their adjustment process.

Providing Transportation

Refugee families are frequently large. They can, for example, have nine, ten, eleven, or more members. They often require transportation assistance at the start of their resettlement process, especially if they have not purchased a car or learned how to use public transportation. Transportation assistance will enable them to move around the city, attend events, and engage in basic activities.

Making Appointments

When our refugee friends are not yet fluent in the local language, they will require assistance from people willing to make appointments with doctors, dentists, and government officials on their behalf. Making phone calls and setting up appointments is another important way to help the refugee community. In some cases, accompanying them to appointments can be extremely beneficial in helping them to progress in their new living context.

Making Connections

Another practical way to serve the refugees in our community is to connect them with people who can assist them. For example, it is vital to connect them with job placement services in their new context. Because there are so many areas of need in a refugee ministry, connecting the right people to the refugee community is the most effective way to carry out the work. Connecting our refugee friends with a group of people is a vital way of sharing the workload and providing the appropriate services to the refugee community.

Offering Friendship

Many refugees come from communities where friendships are highly valued. When they begin their journey in a new context, they frequently do not have anyone to call a friend. Finding people who are willing to extend friendship will make a significant difference in their lives. One simple way to do this is to visit them in their homes and receive their gift of hospitality. A supportive community where they can relate and form new relationships is essential for many reasons, among them providing support as they overcome the traumatic experiences that led to their refugee status.

Presenting the Gospel

Many biblical passages give us firm assurance that Christians are commanded to share their faith with non-Christians. Consequently, when we share the gospel with our refugee friends, we do so primarily out of obedience to our Lord. Additionally, sharing the gospel is fundamental in a holistic approach because we see our refugee friends as individuals with a body, soul, and spirit. Therefore, we want them to be transformed in every way and to enjoy the new life that Christ has prepared for them.

Conclusion

Given the millions of refugees scattered around the globe, we, as followers of Jesus, need to keep in mind our identity and position in this world. As people who have found refuge in Christ and have become citizens of God's kingdom, we must identify with those in exile and welcome them into the place where God has given us temporary residence. May our effort produce experiences like those of Abdu Ali, who, amid pain and suffering, not only found a place of refuge in a strange land but an opportunity for a new life in Christ Jesus.

Bibliography

Hébert, Jacques. "The 'With' of Diaspora Missiology: The Impact of Kinship, Honor, and Hospitality on the Future of Missionary Training, Sending, and Partnership." Accessed March 10, 2019. https://nextmove.net/old/uploads/Kinnship-Bridging-hebert.pdf.

Tira, Sadiri Joy, and Darrell Jackson. "Responding to the Phenomenon of Migration: Early Proponents of Diaspora Missiology and the Lausanne Movement." In *Scattered and Gathered: A Global Compendium of Diaspora Missiology*, edited by Sadiri Joy Tira and and Tetsunao Yamamori, 93–104. Carlisle, UK: Langham, 2020.

UNHCR. "Global Trends 2021." Accessed January 15, 2023. *The UN Refugee Agency*. https://www.unhcr.org/62a9d1494/global-trends-report-2021.

UNHCR. "Refugee Data Finder." Accessed January 15, 2023. *The UN Refugee Agency*. https://www.unhcr.org/refugee-statistics.

Yang, Jenny Hwang. "Immigrants in the USA: A Missional Opportunity." In *Global Diasporas and Mission*, edited by Chandler H. Im and Amos Young, 148–57. Oxford: Regnum, 2014.

Further Reading

de Oliveira, Jairo. *Changing Stories: Responding to the Refugee Crisis Based on Biblical Theory and Practice*. Eugene: Wipf & Stock, 2020.

George, Sam, and Miriam Adeney, eds. *Refugee Diaspora: Missions amid the Greatest Humanitarian Crisis of the World*. Littleton, CO: William Carey Publishing, 2018. Kindle.

Payne, J. D. *Strangers Next Door: Immigration, Migration and Mission*. Downers Grove, IL: InterVarsity Press, 2012.

Soerens, Matthew, and Jenny Hwang Yang. *Welcoming the Stranger: Justice, Compassion & Truth in the Immigration Debate*. Downers Grove, IL: InterVarsity Press, 2010.

Tira, Sadiri Joy, and Tetsunao Yamamori, eds. *Scattered and Gathered: A Global Compendium of Diaspora Missiology*. Carlisle, UK: Langham, 2020.

Part Five

The People of Praise, Word, and Deed in Mission

Living in a radically globalizing world means that mission practitioners encounter rapidly shifting dynamics in regard to cultural changes and intercultural interaction when engaging in God's mission. Awareness of these dynamics is essential to working effectively and empathetically with others who have different backgrounds but preach the same gospel, which proclaims that "there is neither Greek nor Jew, there is neither slave nor free, there is no male and female, for you are all one in Christ Jesus" (Gal 3:28 ESV).

In this section, we move on from a missional past that too often considered mission to be a one-way flow from the West to the rest and reframe the discussion more broadly as mission from everywhere to everywhere, working together to obey the Great Commission to make disciples of all nations while also obeying the great commandment to love one another well in the process.

Chapter 17

Revitalizing the House Church Tradition

A Viable Path for the Churches in China

Zhiqiu Xu

Introduction

The house church finds its origin in the first three hundred years of church history. It's the most natural structure that characterized pre-Constantine churches. A close study of Romans 16 reveals that before AD 60 there were probably seven to eight church blocks discernable in Rome, all of which were hosted in private houses. These house churches were empowered by the dynamic vitality of the Spirit, spreading all over the coasts of the Mediterranean. These house churches turned the Roman Empire upside down, leaving a long-lasting impact on human civilization.

Since the late 1970s, the house church movement in China has been growing in a model that's very similar to that of the early church. It signifies an indigenous stage of church growth that reflects more of the natural principles of the early church. However, the newly emerged indigenous church movement is now heavily influenced by Western denominations and institutions. Consciously or unconsciously, many house churches reach a crossroads where the choice must be made between continuing to grow as house churches or adopting the Western institutionalized model. It is a choice between the early church paradigm and the post-modern, Western denominational paradigm. This chapter discusses the pros and cons of these models with the purpose of reaffirming the house church model as the one that best fits the contemporary Chinese church.

My Story

I was born in the early 1970s in a village about fifty kilometers north of Shanghai. I became a Christian at the age of seventeen by listening to a radio program, "The Hour of Decision," hosted by the Billy Graham ministry. The program was prepared in Hong Kong and broadcast from Guam. After my college entrance exam in 1989, I went to Beijing for undergraduate and graduate studies. During my graduate years, I attended a house church there called Shouwang. The founder and pastor of the church mentored and prepared me for full-time ministry. Though ethnically Korean, the Pastor is a Chinese citizen.

Like many Korean pastors, he had a dream of building up a mega church, a church larger than the Yoido Full Gospel Church in Seoul, which had one million members at its peak. Often, the pastor shared his vision by walking around large parcels of land. Nevertheless, this mega church dream clashed head-on with the political agenda of the government, whose goals were to minimize, contain, and eventually dissolve the church. The clashes between the state and church led to numerous instances of confrontation, harassment, and persecution. In spite of this, the pastor's mega church dream persisted. He and the church board decided to go public by purchasing the whole floor of a commercial building in Beijing. The church was denied access to the building. The pastor reacted by leading the congregation into a park to conduct outdoor services. I vividly remember the first outdoor worship service. The congregation stood together on an early winter morning as he delivered a heart-warming message—quite a symbol of the churches in China.

After that, persecution escalated. Beginning in June 2011, several dozen church members were detained every week and forced to sign a disavowal of their membership with Shouwang before being released. Six church leaders were placed under house arrest without any court documentation. The Beijing police mobilized forty-five hundred officers to surveil the outdoor service. They blocked the homes of about five hundred church members to prevent the church from gathering.

From 2011 to 2021, the pastor and his wife were confined to house arrest. I paid them a visit in 2016. While we had some very delightful conversation, on the other side of the door were policemen and security officers guarding the entrance around the clock. These symbols depict the reality of the relationship between church and state in China. How will the church survive and thrive under that condition? Is there a viable path for the churches in China?

Lessons from the Early Church

The contemporary church in China is similar to the early church in the Roman Empire in that the present Chinese church lives under a hostile regime, is deprived of rights and gathers in household settings. Also like the early church, the church in China is fast growing and loves the Lord. The church in China has a lot to learn from the early church. The early church not only survived the Roman Empire's harsh persecutions but it also grew exponentially, turning the world upside down.

From the year AD 33 to 311, the early church sustained various waves of persecution. Generally, they could not worship publicly because they were often forbidden to own property. The contemporary household churches in China, including Shouwang, are experiencing similar clashes between the church and the state. Shouwang's attempted shift from being a house church to an institutional church accelerated the conflict.

Early Household Churches in Romans 16

In Romans 16, the Apostle Paul offers us a peek into the clusters of local household churches in first-century Rome. Popular scholarly opinion affirms that Paul wrote Romans around AD 57 from Corinth. The letter was carried to Rome by Phoebe, a *diakonos* from the church of Cenchrea near Corinth. If she arrived on a Sunday, there would have been a worship gathering in a home. It would have begun with a meal (a Love Feast), followed by a celebration of the Lord's Supper, hymn singing, and a time of teaching and discussion.[1] On this day, Phoebe would have shared Paul's letter. Perhaps clusters of house churches from the area gathered to hear Paul's words.

The following excerpts from Romans 16 (NASB) provide more of a window into that first-century house church gathering.

> I recommend to you our sister Phoebe, who is a servant of the church which is at Cenchrea ... Greet Prisca and Aquila, my fellow workers in Christ Jesus, who risked their own necks for my life, to whom not only do I give thanks, but also all the churches of the Gentiles; also greet the church that is in their house. Greet Epaenetus, my beloved, who is the first convert to Christ from Asia. Greet Mary, who has worked hard for you. Greet Andronicus and Junia, my kinsfolk and my fellow prisoners, who are outstanding in the view of the apostles, who also were in Christ before me. Greet Ampliatus, my beloved in the Lord. Greet Urbanus, our fellow worker in Christ, and Stachys my beloved. Greet Apelles, the approved in Christ. Greet those who are of the household of Aristobulus. Greet Herodion, my kinsman. Greet those of the household of Narcissus, who are in the Lord. Greet Tryphaena and Tryphosa, workers in the Lord. Greet Persis the beloved, who has worked

---

1 Ramsaran, "Paul and Maxims," 124.

hard in the Lord. Greet Rufus, a choice man in the Lord, also his mother and mine. Greet Asyncritus, Phlegon, Hermes, Patrobas, Hermas, and the brothers and sisters with them. Greet Philologus and Julia, Nereus and his sister, and Olympas, and all the saints who are with them. Greet one another with a holy kiss. All the churches of Christ greet you.

Following the passage closely, Paul appears to greet house churches according to their locations within the city. He greets multiple house church leaders, their families, and the groups meeting in their homes. These were authentic, established churches meeting in private homes.

In *From Paul to Valentinus*, Peter Lampe points out that by the mid AD 50s, Rome had seven or eight church blocks.[2] The blocks of churches functioned as clusters. Early on, there were clusters of two to three house churches that later expanded to ten to fifteen churches in a cluster. In each house church, attendance averaged between twenty-five and forty worshippers, though some larger groups ranged between fifty and seventy members. Though the house churches in a network were relatively independent, some practices knit them together, such as sharing the Eucharist, sharing food from house to house, and sharing with the needy in the community outside of the house churches. In short, the early churches were house churches connected to other house churches in a network.

Early Churches as a Blockchain Model

To use a modern banking analogy, as a network of house churches, the early church embodied a "blockchain" model. This model can be observed in at least four ways. First, the early church grew naturally with a decentralized structure. As we just observed in Romans 16, the house church blocks did not have a centralized headquarters. The church spread all over the districts within the city and all over the cities in the Roman Empire. Not only was the structure of the early church decentralized, but the gospel message was transmitted in a decentralized manner. Jesus did not entrust his message and mission to just one person; he chose twelve. The risen Lord appeared on multiple occasions to a multitude of people. At Pentecost, the Holy Spirit baptized people from every corner of the empire, enabling them to speak in a variety of tongues. The Great Commission was given to every Christian, commissioning all believers to preach the gospel message in all of the world.

Second, these early decentralized churches shared a common and essential message. House churches strove to be faithful to the authentic

---

2 Lampe, *From Paul to Valentinus*, 359–61.

gospel message by fighting against a variety of heresies. In fact, part of Paul's purpose for writing Romans was to clarify the central message of justification by faith in Jesus Christ.

Third, the gospel message is universal; it can be verified between the house church blocks to ensure its authenticity. This nature of verifiability accounted for the formation of early church creeds and the canonicity of the New Testament books. One of the criteria for a book to be accepted into New Testament canon was that its authority was widely recognized and universally accepted.

Fourth, the early house churches multiplied exponentially in all directions. Peter and Paul were just two representatives of multiple lines of church multiplication. Others included Barnabas's line after he parted ways with Paul, John's line in Ephesus, Mark's in Egypt, and Thomas's line in India.

Contemporary Churches in China

If the early church managed to survive and even thrive under the cruel persecution of the Roman Empire, it must have something to teach the contemporary church in China. From a historical viewpoint, the real danger to the Chinese church has not come from external persecution, but from internal challenges. Church leaders have lost a clear vision. They've become disoriented and pursued wrong models and paradigms for ministry.

Following the Communist Party's twentieth congressional meeting, which gave the present leader a lifetime term, China is on its way to becoming a giant North Korea. It's likely that China will go through a second wave of Maoist Cultural Revolution, which purged intellectual and cultural leaders from society. The post-pandemic policy deprives people of the right to gather. Digital surveillance prevents any gathering beyond the size of a family. This reality makes the mega church vision nearly impossible.

From an economic perspective, skyrocketing rental costs take a heavy toll on urban church groups that followed the trend of relocating from households to commercial buildings. For instance, before being forced to close, the Zion Church in Beijing rented a floor in a commercial building.[3] The annual rental cost was about three million Chinese Yuan, which amounted to three-quarters of the church's annual budget. With most of their resources going to rent, there was very little left for strategic development—for discipleship training, social ministry, or global mission sending. Also, since pastors and staff members are severely

---

3 "China Bans Zion."

underpaid, few young Christians dare to step into full-time ministry. Even if they desired to enter full-time ministries, their parents would forbid it.

Adopting an institutional model has actually slowed the growth of the Chinese church. Between the late 1970s and the year 2000, the Chinese house church movement experienced a golden age of sorts. Household churches require few or no full-time professionals to run the church. Every church member engaged in various church ministries. Christians in house churches are usually more fervent in spreading the gospel. In my personal experience, churches were healthier when they avoided an institutional model.

The contemporary churches in China are encountering a lot of difficulties. The increased political pressure is pushing the churches back into houses. The anti-pandemic policy imposes strict limits on social gatherings, forcing the churches to gather in smaller groups. Various episodes in church history testify that a hostile political and social environment may actually help the church to grow and spread faster. When the first-century Jerusalem church suffered severe persecution, the disciples scattered in all directions. They involuntarily fulfilled the Great Commission which commanded them to go. Practically speaking, the house church model's spontaneity offers a viable path for the contemporary Chinese churches to flourish among these challenges.

Conclusion: Advantages of the House Church Model

The early church household model offers the contemporary Chinese churches multiple advantages. First, the local church as a family of families that gather in the household setting is a recovery of the historic Chinese household church, which has been resilient and effective. Though the government may limit gatherings to fifty, or even just twenty people, churches this size are healthier and more vital than institutional-style churches. Second, by moving churches from rented spaces back to family dwellings, the churches save a great deal on operational costs. There is very little cost for a church when it meets in a private home.

Third, the family environment enhances fellowship within the local church. Since the beginnings of the Christian movement, churches have operated on the principles of being a spiritual family. From the New Testament texts, churches were households built around the family structure. A family model remains strong even in the face of pressure from a dictatorial regime. The family structure also encourages natural growth through evangelism and mission. It prevents the silent exodus of young people from the church because of persecution.

Fourth, the household model encourages all members of the church to discover their spiritual gifts and to exercise them in various ministries. This contrasts with the institutional model where only professional ministers (pastors, elders, music leaders) have opportunities to practice their gifts. In other words, the household model excels in discipleship, which produces more mature Christians.

In short, the house church model of the early church is very meaningful for the Chinese church today. It was a movement birthed and empowered by the Holy Spirit. Following the natural structure of early Roman cities, house churches multiplied in many directions. There is an urgent need for churches in China and worldwide, especially those under persecution, to recover the early house church model to promote genuine fellowship, healthy structures, and another wave of growth.

Bibliography

"China Bans Zion, Beijing's Biggest House Church." *Christianity Today*, September 10, 2018. https://www.christianitytoday.com/news/2018/september/china-bans-zion-beijing-house-church-surveillance-ezra-jin.html.

Lampe, Peter. *From Paul to Valentinus: Christians at Rome in the First Two Centuries*. Minneapolis: Fortress, 2003.

Ramsaran, R. A. "Paul and Maxims." In *Paul in the Greco-Roman World: A Handbook*, edited by J. P. Sampley, 124. London: T&T Clark, 2003.

Chapter 18

From South to North

Sub-Saharans in the Mission of God

William A. Brown

Introduction

I was recently invited to dinner to celebrate the birthday of one of my dearest friends and colleagues, Freddy. After the main course, Freddy, a Congolese, asked our Tunisian server to take a picture of us with his smartphone. As soon as the waiter took the photo, Freddy looked at his phone (and his face in the picture) with a look of horror. Reluctantly, he showed us the picture. While one could easily see that Bernard and I were happy, Freddy was invisible! The dim setting of the restaurant and Freddy's dark black skin gave the impression that he was not there at all.

This humorous incident (we laughed for over twenty minutes) illustrates how sub-Saharan Africans in the mission of God are often considered by the evangelical church in the West: They are present but largely invisible. Compared to global ambassadors in the North, sub-Saharans are the minority. Yet, statistics show that the future of the global mission force is south of the Sahara Desert. In 2017, the Pew Research Center estimated that by 2060, four of every ten Christians will be from sub-Saharan Africa.[1] As we reflect on the hope of gospel-driven transformation among the least-reached communities of our world, we in the West must intentionally consider the unique position of our sub-Saharan brothers and sisters in the global mission enterprise.

This chapter addresses the role of sub-Saharan cross-cultural workers in the north of Africa. We'll briefly look at the history of the "Go North" movement and then examine some of the strengths and challenges of the sub-Saharan missionary community. We'll finish by offering some applications.

---

1 McClendon, "Sub-Saharan Africa."

Our North African Experience

My family and I arrived in North Africa in 2002 to pastor a French-speaking international church in the center of Tunis. Freddy, mentioned in the story above, arrived in 2003 at roughly the same time as the African Development Bank from war-worn Cote d'Ivoire. The next year, our church welcomed another worker from East Africa. Little by little, God began bringing other sub-Saharans to North Africa. Some heard about the needs in North Africa while still in their own countries. Others experienced the need firsthand as international students in North Africa and decided to stay.[2] Today we have at least sixteen cross-cultural workers from Benin, Gabon, Ivory Coast, Rwanda, Burundi, Ethiopia, Congo (Brazzaville) and Congo (DRC). Next year we expect a family from Burkina Faso to join us, as well as an intern from Togo. While our perspectives are limited, our experience confirms the movement of God from south to north.

MANI—Movement for African National Initiatives

Though cross-cultural engagement has been part of the church in Africa for centuries, a renewed push to go north has occurred in the last twenty years. Much of this effort has been facilitated through MANI. According to their website, "MANI is an African movement, a network of networks and African National Initiatives, focused on catalyzing African National Initiatives and mobilizing the resources of the body of Christ in Africa for the fulfillment of the Great Commission."[3]

With the growing movements for independence in Africa in the 1960s, missionaries from the West began leaving more room for African nationals to lead from that time forward. Evangelical leaders in countries like Ghana, Nigeria, and the Democratic Republic of Congo began taking ownership for the evangelism and discipleship of their countries. Movements such as Discipling A Whole Nation (DAWN) and AD 2000 and Beyond included efforts from different African countries. The 1997 Global Consultation on World Evangelism (GCOWE) in South Africa, which witnessed the forming of African National Initiatives, was the first global consultation in recent history in which over half of the delegates were from the African continent.

To commemorate the close of the work of AD 2000 and Beyond, a congress was planned in Jerusalem. At the last minute, Celebrate Messiah

---

2 French is the second language in Mauritania, Algeria, Morocco, and Tunisia. These countries welcome thousands of students per year from French-speaking Africa.

3 "(MANI) – An Overview."

2000, which was to welcome nearly four thousand delegates, was cancelled. Nevertheless, over three hundred delegates from thirty-six different African countries still believed that God wanted them to meet. This was the birth of MANI.

Five years after its founding, MANI convened a consultation in Nairobi, Kenya. MANI 2006 highlighted, among other issues, the priority of data among the unreached communities on the continent. Five years later, in Abuja, Nigeria, over six hundred delegates gathered to hear the sobering feedback. While some countries south of the Sahara, such as Nigeria and Kenya, count Christians in the millions, others in the northern band of Africa from Senegal to Somalia count believers in the hundreds or even dozens. At MANI 2011, the clarion call was clear: "Go North."

Why Africans Are Well-Suited to "Go North"

When I mention to Western friends that I am involved in mobilizing and receiving sub-Saharan Africans for work in the north, some are surprised. The first things they think of are the challenges. While there are some uncontested obstacles which we'll address later on, there are also reasons why sub-Saharans are well positioned to "Go North."[4]

The first reason is the sheer numerical strength of the church in sub-Saharan Africa. Conservative estimates place the number of evangelicals at 180 million. According to the Joshua Project, 33 percent of Rwanda and 49 percent of Kenya are evangelical, to name just two sub-Saharan African countries.[5]

A second asset of sub-Saharan workers is the strength of their religious background. Many of them have lived with Muslims and know the Muslim context. We have seen this strength especially with workers from countries with a Christian minority. Isaiah, a Christian student leader from Conakry, Guinea, was not thrown off by the theological questions of his Muslim classmates in North Africa; he was used to them. Adam, a cross-cultural worker from Niger, already knew how to defend his faith when he showed up for a three-month internship with our church.

A third strength of the African church is her passion for prayer and heightened awareness of spiritual warfare. Anyone who has lived in sub-Saharan Africa understands this dynamic. All night or all weekend prayer vigils along with days (or weeks) of fasting are normal for churches.

---

4 I am deeply indebted to a colleague for this list. In his unpublished paper from Fuller Seminary, he lists thirteen reasons that sub-Saharans are well suited to go north.

5 "Africa Country and People."

Deliverance ministries are a common part of church life. Several years ago, a North African Muslim friend of mine, Jamil, came to me for help. He sincerely believed that he had been cursed for discontinuing annual food offerings to a Muslim Sufi saint. When I told him that I could pray for him, he insisted on seeing one of my sub-Saharan colleagues whom he had never met. "You don't understand curses, William. Africans do."

Stealth is a fourth quality that sub-Saharans possess. In some towns, Westerners stick out like a sore thumb; at times, they are targeted. Sub-Saharan students, by contrast, can fly under the radar. In one isolated area of North Africa with more than two hundred thousand people, Western missionaries would raise eyebrows in the community. The only Christ-followers there are twenty-six sub-Saharan students who live out their faith freely.

A fifth advantage for sub-Saharans is their linguistic strength. Most Africans speak at least two languages. They are used to new languages. One cross-cultural worker from East Africa who works with us speaks four languages. Learning Arabic or Amazigh is just adding another one to the list.

Sub-Saharan Africans generally possess a sixth strength as well—cultural awareness. This strength plays out in at least two ways in North Africa. Africans, whether from the north or the south, are from collective cultures. This trait stands in contrast to the individualist thinking more common in the West. In that respect, sub-Saharans understand their North African counterparts. A second common cultural trait is that Africans, from the north and the south, generally have high power distance. They give great esteem to people in authority and honor the hierarchical social systems.

In a similar vein, a seventh advantage for sub-Saharans is common colonial and protectorate baggage. North Africans and most of their sub-Saharan cousins share a history of being colonized by foreign entities, many by France. As a result, empathy exists between the two groups that Westerners have difficulty understanding. I vividly recall expressing my frustration to my Congolese colleague regarding a North African church leader's attitude towards an American pastor. My Congolese co-worker replied, "You cannot understand, William, because you don't know what it's like to be colonized."

Challenges for Sub-Saharan Workers

While we affirm the unique ways that sub-Saharans are equipped to go north, one cannot deny that there are challenges as well. I have talked with some American Christians who wonder if, given these obstacles, the task of sub-Saharans going north is even worth it.

At the top of the list of hurdles is prejudice and racism against blacks. This struggle is a reoccurring story all over North Africa. Acts of racial violence in Tunisia became so bad that a law was passed in 2018 against racial discrimination. Americans and Europeans are often treated with greater respect by the police or government than the North African national. At the bottom of the totem pole are black Africans. Black members of our church have been spat on, yelled at, and even beaten.

The second obstacle for sub-Saharan workers in the North is the lack of sustainable financing. The models that are often used in the West that require raising one's own support from one's church network are not always reproducible. A village church in Burundi cannot give in proportion to what a white, suburban church in Atlanta can donate. Furthermore, the support required by Western organizations seems exorbitant to our brothers and sisters from the Global South. As an American, I pay more per month for health insurance than the entire support package for some of my co-workers. Some organizations, such as Mediterranean Partners, strive to help support non-Western workers without creating dependency.

A third challenge for sub-Saharans is the visa issues they encounter because of their low passport power ranking. Passport power ranking reflects the number of countries the passport holder can travel to visa-free or through getting a visa on arrival. This process something many Westerners take for granted. For example, the United States and Canada are ranked third and fourth place respectively. Sub-Saharan countries are at the bottom of the ranking. Cote d'Ivoire is tied for seventy-seventh, and Nigeria is tied for ninetieth, while Nepal, South Sudan, and Ethiopia are tied for ninety-first.[6] Recently, when a Congolese intern from our church returned to Brazzaville to visit her parents, she discovered that the cheapest ticket was through Europe. However, because she could not obtain the required visa, she was forced to buy a more expensive ticket through another African country.

A fourth hurdle is the shortage of member care resources adapted for sub-Saharan workers. This difficulty often means we are using materials made for a Western audience. Furthermore, trained counselors who understand both the unique challenges of sub-Saharan workers and missionary life are rare.

Other challenges abound that are not unique to sub-Saharans but take on a different flavor in the "Go North" movement. There is, for example,

---

6 "Global Passport Power."

the tension of different ministry paradigms. Church structure in Libya is different from Burkina Faso. We could add to these obstacles the potential conflict between the sending church and the missionary regarding the needs of the least-reached and the allotment of finances. The influence of prosperity gospel teaching, the lack of adequate education options for missionary children, and the clash of cultural values on multi-cultural teams are also sources of frustration.

Moving Forward

A basic application of this move of God in Africa is an acute realization that the missionary force is bigger and more diverse than we have imagined. God is using the Global South in ways that some from the West could never have imagined. We from the West are partners and co-laborers together with Burundian, Togolese, and Malagasy brothers and sisters with Christ in his field. That awareness should encourage humility on our part.

That humility plays out in various ways. When you or your church prays for missionaries, add to your list specific ones sent out by the African church. That may require research if you don't know one. Support an African missionary. A starting point might be the Nigerian Evangelical Mission Association, an umbrella organization that gathers over one hundred fifty mission agencies based in Nigeria and represents over fifteen thousand missionaries.[7] One of these agencies, CAPRO Ministries, sends over seven hundred missionaries and has offices in over twenty countries in Africa.[8] The Faithful Witness program of SIM expressly sends multi-cultural teams, including sub-Saharans, to least-reached communities.[9] A US-based non-profit, Mediterranean Partners, also partners with non-Western workers in North Africa.[10] In the same way that you might financially support one of your friends, consider partnering financially with those from sub-Saharan Africa.

For those who have lived in Africa or are still living there, consider using your training, experience, and gifts to participate in mobilizing and encouraging the African church in her missional endeavor. In the same way that accountants, programmers, intercessors, counselors, and lawyers, are needed in missionary-sending centers around the world, these gifts are needed in African sending centers.

---

7   See further Nigerian Evangelical Mission Association.
8   See further CAPRO Ministries.
9   See further SIM Faithful Witness.
10 See further Mediterranean Partners.

To Westerners living cross-culturally among the least-reached, prayerfully consider how you might join what God is doing in the African church. What can you do to facilitate mobilizing and receiving workers from the Global South? As you look for English teachers, could you expand your recruiting pool to include Kenya and Ghana, for example? Imagine adding an Ivorian programmer to your business along with your North American colleague or a Gabonese to your international church staff.

Our response to the above considerations may reveal some prideful positions on our part as Westerners. This is where the heart work takes place. Do we consider workers from the Global South to be truly equal partners in Jesus's harvest, or has our training and wealth borne subtle attitudes of condescension and even racism? I have met Christian workers ready to serve North African nationals who at the same time completely ignore the presence of sub-Saharan co-laborers. We are members of the same family. Do siblings disregard each other? Dr. Solomon Aryeetey, Founder of Pioneers-Africa, summarizes it this way:

> Contrary to what is widely believed in many evangelical circles, and even in many great centers of theological and missiological thought, the end result of all missionary work is not the planting of churches. Neither is it even the establishment of church-planting movements. The final product is a Bride for a Bridegroom … The Bride of Christ is either adorned with a coat of many colors, or she is not his bride at all. Multicultural, multiracial—one body made up of diverse parts, each with its own specific function which the other segments can never bring to the table. And, "Sebi tafratse" ["with all due respect"], when the tendency in the West is to equate the huge, stunning disparity between them and the rest of the Christian world in terms of wealth and resources, this betrays how utterly worldly these in the West have become.[11]

The not-so-distant future of God's redemptive work in history is found in Africa. How will you joyfully join God in this work?

Bibliography

"Africa Country and People Groups Listings." Joshua Project. Accessed February 1, 2023. https://joshuaproject.net/continents.

Aryeetey, Solomon. "*Sebi Tafratse* (with All Due Respects): A Word to the West from the Rest." Missio Nexus. April 1, 2013. https://missionexus.org/sebi-tafratse-with-all-due-respects-a-word-to-the-west-from-the-rest-2/.

CAPRO Ministries. Accessed February 7, 2023. http://caprousa.org.

---

11 Solomon Aryeetey, "Sebi Tafratse."

"Global Passport Power Rank 2023: Passport Index 2023." Passport Index. Accessed February 1, 2023. https://www.passportindex.org/byRank.php.

"(MANI) – An Overview." Movement for African National Initiatives (MANI). Accessed February 1, 2023. https://maniafrica.com/mani-an-overview/.

McClendon, David. "Sub-Saharan Africa Will Be Home to Growing Shares of the World's Christians and Muslims." Pew Research Center. April 19, 2017. https://www.pewresearch.org/fact-tank/2017/04/19/sub-saharan-africa-will-be-home-to-growing-shares-of-the-worlds-christians-and-muslims/.

Mediterranean Partners. Accessed February 7, 2023. https://mediterraneanpartners.com/.

Nigerian Evangelical Mission Association. Accessed February 7, 2023. http://nemanigeriamissions.org.

SIM Faithful Witness. Accessed February 7, 2023. https://www.sim.org/faithfulwitness.

Further Reading

Escobar, Samuel. *The New Global Mission: The Gospel from Everywhere to Everyone*. Downers Grove, IL: IVP Academic, 2023.

Jenkins, Philip. *The Next Christendom: The Coming of Global Christianity*. Revised edition. New York: Oxford University Press, 2007.

Chapter 19

Lessons Learned on Multicultural Teams

Sean Christensen

During my first year as a missionary, the Haitian director of our Bible college called me into his office. He asked me how I was doing, how my family was doing, and how our adaptation to the new culture was going. Then he explained that his truck was in the shop and that it needed four new tires. He stated he would pay for one tire, I would pay for one, and our two German teammates would pay for the other two. He wasn't demanding this or even asking; just making a statement. And I agreed to do it. I later asked one of my German teammates what he thought about this "request." He shrugged his shoulders and said, "Well, it seems this is what we are doing."

How does this story make you feel? What do you think was going on in this situation? How would you have responded? Of course, it is difficult to judge because you don't know the people involved, how their relationships had been defined up to that point, what is considered normal in Haitian culture, and even what precedents were set by previous foreign missionaries. In the end, my German colleagues and I chose to view it as an expression of love and friendship. I served under this Haitian director for twelve more years during which time we experienced mutual love and respect. But this story highlights just one example of the challenges and complexities one finds when working on multicultural teams.

Competency in the Dynamics of Multicultural Teams

Multicultural mission teams (MCTs) are not new. The Apostle Paul's missionary team included Jews, half-Jews, and Greeks. The Haitian Bible college where I served began in 1936 with Cuban, Haitian, and North American teammates. If this is not a new phenomenon, then why does the future of global missions require proficiency in the dynamics of multicultural teams? Plainly put, the present reality, locally and globally, demands multicultural proficiency in most aspects of life. Global migration, digital communications, and the societal trend in Western cultures to repudiate cultural insensitivities all contribute to more interaction with people from diverse cultures and more frequent exposure to their customs and ideas.

I recently mentioned to a twenty-year-old university student preparing to be a missionary that he will quite likely serve his entire time within multicultural teams. He replied, "Well, I sure hope so!" His desire and expectation reflect global realities. Breuel and Tindall write, "Multicultural churches and missions teams are attractive to Gen Z … Because the new generation is more connected than ever before, they understand the global church more tangibly. Young people are very engaged in diversity, equity, and inclusion. They are very attracted to congregations that are multicultural and multigenerational, and those that give voice to both men and women."[1]

The new generation of missionaries expects to serve on multicultural teams, which means they need the training to augment their desire.

Additionally, since the majority of Christians live in the Global South and many regions of the Global South are actively sending missionaries, the global missionary force is multicultural. Porter writes, "We live in an unprecedented period of mission history. The new paradigm of 'from anywhere to everywhere' is by nature complex, resulting in an increasing need to partner with others for effective ministry."[2] Will missionaries from diverse backgrounds intentionally work together to plant churches among the unreached, bearing witness of the presence and power of the Holy Spirit in these MCTs whose members love and accept one another? Surely, those churches will be better prepared to reproduce in kind, since they have learned from the church planters how to discern biblical absolutes from culturally adapted applications of biblical teaching.

Finally, the trend in Western missions away from paternalistic programs to genuine partnerships in mission endeavors means that proficiency in an MCT setting is needed. A recent Lausanne Global Analysis paper referenced global mission leaders who "assert that the leadership of local mission efforts should be local, with outsiders in a supporting role, a principle which is not new, but which is being accelerated by the COVID pandemic … When recruiters ask what type of workers are needed, I now add: 'People who deeply enjoy making others successful!' Those who come with that passion fit well into the new mission paradigm."[3]

---

1 Breuel and Tindall, "Helping Generation Z Flourish," 17.
2 Porter, "Networks & Global Missions."
3 Rievan, "Are Foreigners Still Needed?"

But how does one successfully collaborate, support, and empower across cultural divides where even "success" is measured differently?

In order to function well on a multicultural team, all of the members need cultural awareness and relational skills, on which I elaborate below. But for effective multicultural *missions* teams, the gospel itself—the life and message of Jesus Christ—holds the answers for a thriving multicultural team that reflects God's character to a watching world. Let us explore these three competencies: cultural awareness, relational skills, and the application of the gospel.

Cultural Awareness

Everyone is naturally ethnocentric. The way one is raised is "normal" for that person, and, by extension, for others in their cultural heritage. The problem with ethnocentrism is that people interpret behaviors through the standards of their own cultural norms. Therefore, members of an MCT tend to assign moral judgment to the behavior of their teammates. Often (but not always), that interpretation is a misunderstanding. Evelyn and Richard Hibbert write:

> Diversity has a detrimental effect on team functioning in the early stages of forming and norming. The initial period of turmoil at the start of a new multicultural team is much greater than in the monocultural team ... There are greater initial difficulties in problem solving and greater potential for conflict in negotiating tasks and processes ... Team members commonly misinterpret what their teammates are saying, and this slows the team's progress.[4]

These obstacles of misunderstanding can be overcome, in part, through a better awareness of the kinds of differences that exist between the cultures represented on the team. Four recent books explain some of the opposing cultural traits that one can expect to encounter on a multicultural team.

Erin Meyer, The Culture Map[5]

In Meyer's book, she lists eight significant areas of life and work that are culturally driven. The greater the difference in a given area, the greater potential that area has to create conflict on the team. For example,

---

4 Hibbert, *Leading Multicultural Teams*, 57.

5 A Harvard Business Review article explains the various cultural traits that Erin Meyer researched: Meyer, "Navigating the Cultural Minefield." Additionally, HBR has a free online assessment entitled "What's Your Cultural Profile?" based upon the eight scales Erin Meyer explains in her book, "The Culture Map."

members of Culture A tend to value giving direct negative feedback while members of Culture B prefer to provide negative feedback in more subtle ways. Teammates from Culture A can be perceived as rude and uncaring by teammates from Culture B, whereas Culture A teammates might view their teammates from Culture B as insincere or cowardly.

Cultural differences are often highlighted in decision-making, in the expectations placed on leaders, and in the ways trust is built. On the "Trusting" scale, cultures vary on building trust primarily based upon competencies or primarily based upon personal relationships. Before I learned about Meyer's categories, I experienced an unexpected conflict regarding trust.

One of our teammates in Haiti was a European who grew up in the former Soviet Union. As field director, I had shared publicly a prayer request about a missionary candidate coming to visit this colleague's training institution. She confronted me on my decision, stating, "I can't trust you now because you shared that publicly without asking me first." I realized I had a lot to learn about direct negative feedback, confrontational disagreement, and the bases upon which trust is built. As I learned more, and shared these cultural differences with my colleague, our working relationship improved significantly.

Geert Hofstede, Cultures and Organizations[6]

Hofstede similarly elaborates on six other areas of cultural difference affecting behavior and attitudes. Meyer's research on the "Leading" scale was based, in part, on Hofstede's findings on his "Power Distance" scale. This scale describes the relative relational distance that is expected between people of greater and lower prestige or authority.

I recently spoke to a newly appointed missionary from Australia. His family was preparing to visit several fields to consider for their ministry location. He wanted to understand what we meant by accountability—a strong value in our organization—because many of our field directors are American. He knows that the American leadership style keeps a higher power distance than the Australian style. I commended him on his cultural insight and told him that every team has to form their own team culture, which requires flexibility from everyone. Being aware of these cultural differences can help a team clarify and agree upon how they will resolve conflicts, make decisions, give feedback, and build trust.

---

6 See the country comparison graphs on these cultural scales at Hofstede's website.

Jayson Georges, The 3-D Gospel[7]

Georges's *The 3-D Gospel* is a primer on three "operating systems" that shape the moral consciences, social interactions and spiritual sensitivities in a culture. He asserts that cultural worldviews are shaped primarily by one of three pursuits: (1) to gain innocence and avoid guilt; (2) to gain honor and avoid shame; or (3) to gain power and avoid fear. He then cogently exposits the Scriptures to show that the gospel of Christ answers all of these concerns.

A Malaysian friend first introduced me to the concept that every culture emphasizes one of these three worldviews. Later, during a study sabbatical, I read *The 3-D Gospel*, plus a few other books, that helped me better understand Haitian society, spirituality, and the Haitian conscience. The Haitian director of the Bible college, whom I mentioned in the opening, asked me what I was learning in my reading. I told him that one thing I now realize is that Haitians value relationships more than money. He grinned widely, chuckled to himself, and then said, "Thank you! Thank you! You got it!" Over the next five years, I heard him repeat my comments to other Haitian church leaders as an example of a missionary who made the effort to understand their host culture more deeply.

Jayson Georges, Ministering in Patronage Cultures

In *Ministering in Patronage Cultures*, Georges explains that systems of patronage are common in most of the world, and these systems can work in both healthy and corrupt ways. He shows how God, in the Old Testament, and Christ, in the New Testament, act as patrons in their roles as Savior and King. Because many missionaries work within institutions in developing countries, Georges's explanations are very helpful.

In Haiti, and in other developing countries, one common frustration emerges from the different expectations relating to patronage that are placed on institutions and their directors. Georges writes: "Institutions allow Western individuals to access resources apart from patronage networks. Patronage becomes essential when such formal institutions are weak—or absent ... Attaching oneself to a patron is the most realistic way to survive and move ahead in life."[8]

---

7 Georges offers a free online assessment based on the three paradigms at The Culture Test website.

8 Georges, *Ministering in Patronage Cultures*, 19.

What expectations for health or life insurance or educational scholarships will Cameroonian missionaries have of the Western mission agency with whom they are partnering? What will they expect of a Canadian team leader? How will an American teammate react when she realizes her Haitian teammate is giving her gifts and doing her favors with the expectation of reciprocity well above the monetary value of those gifts? In patronage systems, everything is relational and "without reciprocity, then there is no relationship."[9]

One step beyond identifying the *what* and the *how* of cultural behavior, is to be curious enough to understand the *why*. There are reasons why a society functions the way it does. What seems ridiculous and dysfunctional at first glance will begin to make sense as you observe, listen, and involve yourself in the lives of others.

Relationship Skills

When we talk about multicultural teams in missions, we are really talking about people—teammates, their networks of family, supporters, mentors, and the recipients of their ministries. Those outside relationships are sure to affect the internal relationships on a team. I found that my Haitian team leader intuitively understood this. He asked about my family and other relationships regularly. One factor that contributed to the overall success of our MCT was that he was willing to put in the time and effort in the early stages of our team's formation to build familiarity and trust. We ate together, visited tourist attractions together, went to government offices together, visited each other's homes, and we prayed for each other's needs. Without having benefited from formal training on multicultural team leadership, this brother in Christ did it right. The Hibberts note:

> The finite time and energy of the MCT leader, especially during the early stages of team life, will be almost completely utilized in the interpersonal processes of building good team relationships and a strong team community. The team leader will have minimal time or energy left to focus on the tasks and goals of the team ... As cultural value differences may be difficult, and in some cases impossible, to reconcile, the MCT leader has to be a skilled negotiator and mediator who can facilitate a process that enables all team members to agree on a unique set of team values that will form the foundation for a healthy team community.[10]

---

9   Del Chinchen, quoted in Georges, *Ministering in Patronage Cultures*, 122.
10 Hibbert, *Leading Multicultural Teams*, 66.

If I had to choose one trait and one skill to best serve a leader or member of an MCT, the trait would be *humility*, and the skill, *listening*. Across the globe, North Americans are not always known for being strong in either of these, even though they are biblical values. I was in an online working group with two Germans, two Americans, and one Filipino. The four Westerners freely shared our ideas on how we could better train missionaries in the necessary skills to serve on an MCT. Sometimes we interrupted each other in our robust dialogue. All the while, our Filipino teammate remained silent. Finally, I asked him to share his thoughts. He smiled and contributed his unique and invaluable perspective.

Scripture further challenges us to be good listeners and humble servants. James writes, "Know this, my beloved brothers: let every person be quick to hear, slow to speak, slow to anger" (Jas 1:19 ESV). In many cultures, these three characteristics are considered primary virtues. To this, Paul adds, "Do nothing from selfish ambition or conceit, but in humility count others more significant than yourselves" (Phil 2:3 ESV). Humility means that I do not assume that my way must be the best way. The Hibberts write, an "MCT needs to be a safe enough place that members feel free to challenge each other's assumptions and attitudes and query why they do things the way they do without feeling that one culture will necessarily overrule."[11] When the members of an MCT can humbly learn from Jesus together, they have reached a healthy level of maturity.

The Application of the Gospel

The difference between making an MCT *function* and making it *thrive* for God's purposes is applying the gospel—the message of Jesus Christ. Let us consider three overlapping aspects of the gospel along with their applications on MCTs:

Aspect	Description	Application
Who Jesus is	Member of the Trinity	Love and Fellowship (*Koinonia*)
What Jesus did	Incarnation and Sacrifice	Incarnational and Sacrificial (*Kenosis*)
What Jesus has given us	Glory	Service from Fullness

---

11 Hibbert, *Leading Multicultural Teams*, 66.

Jesus said that whoever has seen him has seen the Father (John 14:9 ESV) and that he and the Father are one (John 10:30). As Jesus trained his apostles (missionaries), he methodically pulled them into the loving unity of the Trinity. Jesus's final training session with them included these words, "*As the Father has loved me,* so have I loved you. Abide in my love ... This is my commandment, that you love one another as I have loved you" (John 15:9, 12 ESV, emphasis mine). "By this all people will know that you are my disciples, if you have love for one another" (John 13:35 ESV). We are more than partners; we are multicultural brothers and sisters in Christ. With the love of our heavenly Father uniting us to himself, and in communion with one another, we are propelled together on his mission to the lost world.

Though most Christians would affirm that we are a family, putting this into practice on a MCT can be challenging. Gwinner notes, "People from task-oriented cultures will likely initiate a partnership or view an existing partnership in the light of the task. What are we going to do? What is the mission we will accomplish? They need to be aware that people from collective cultures also value the task, but they do not define themselves with what they do and they most often will value the relationship more than the task."[12]

The way such *koinonia* is lived out is through *kenosis*, self-denial. Jesus was the model for incarnational mission, and we are called to imitate him (Eph 5:1, 2 ESV). Paul exhorted the church: "have this mind among yourselves, which is yours in Christ Jesus, who, though he was in the form of God, did not count equality with God a thing to be grasped, but emptied himself, by taking the form of a servant, being born in the likeness of men" (Phil 2:5–7 ESV). Jesus remained God while he lived in human flesh. Though MCT members remain who they are, as Jesus deprived himself of divine privileges to take on human limitations and weaknesses (Heb 2:10–18 ESV), MCT members also surrender their cultural preferences in deference to their teammates. While each member surrenders part of their culture, they also contribute to the overall team culture out of love for Christ and for the sake of Christ's mission.

Where do we find the strength to deny ourselves in a loving way? Jesus supplies the inner power to love sacrificially. Jesus prayed in the hearing of his disciples, "*The glory that you have given me* I have given to them, that they may be one even as we are one, I in them and you in me, that they may become perfectly one, so that the world may know that you sent me"

---

12 Gwinner, "More than Partnership," 158.

(John 17:22–23 ESV, emphasis mine). The glory that Jesus has given to every believer makes human applause insignificant and selfish ambitions unthinkable. It inspires the members of an MCT to submit to one another joyfully. Such unity is a vibrant witness to a watching world!

Conclusion

As we ponder the future of global mission, multicultural teams will continue to be a characteristic of the people of God on mission. Cross-cultural ministry is always difficult, and it can even be more challenging when part of the cross-cultural experience is relating to our own teammates. However, the competencies of cultural awareness, relational skills, and the application of the gospel of Christ are three means by which multicultural mission teams can function effectively, and even thrive, for the glory of God and his redemptive mission in this world.

Bibliography

Breuel, René, Sarah Breuel, and Mary Tindall. "Helping Generation Z Flourish and Be Catalysts for God's Mission." *Evangelical Missions Quarterly* 58, no. 4 (Oct–Dec 2022): 14–17.

Georges, Jayson. *The 3-D Gospel: Ministry in Guilt, Shame, and Fear Cultures*. N.p.: Timē Press, 2017.

Georges, Jayson. "The Culture Test." Online assessment. http://theculturetest.com/.

Georges, Jayson. *Ministering in Patronage Cultures: Biblical Models and Missional Implications*. Downers Grove, IL: InterVarsity Press, 2019.

Gwinner, Detlef. "More than Partnership: A Contextual Model of an Organic-Complementary Communion in World Mission under Consideration of Kenosis." PhD diss., University of South Africa, 2013. https://uir.unisa.ac.za/bitstream/handle/10500/13097/thesis_gwinner_d.pdf.

Hibbert, Evelyn, and Richard Hibbert. *Leading Multicultural Teams*. Pasadena, CA: William Carey Publishing, 2014.

Hofstede, Geert, Gert Jan Hofstede, and Michael Minkov. *Cultures and Organizations: Software of the Mind*. 3rd ed. New York: McGraw Hill, 2010.

Hofstede, Geert. "Country Comparison Graphs." https://geerthofstede.com/country-comparison-graphs/.

Meyer, Erin. *The Culture Map: Decoding How People Think, Lead, and Get Things Done Across Cultures*. New York: PublicAffairs, 2014.

Meyer, Erin. "Navigating the Cultural Minefield." *Harvard Business Review*, May 2014. https://hbr.org/2014/05/navigating-the-cultural-minefield.

Meyer, Erin. "What's Your Cultural Profile?" *Harvard Business Review*, August 14, 2014. Online Assessment. https://hbr.org/2014/08/whats-your-cultural-profile.

Porter, Eldon. "Networks & Global Missions: A Dance Floor and a Country Home." *Mission Frontiers* 39, no. 2 (March/April 2017): 19–22. http://www.missionfrontiers.org/issue/article/networks-global-missions.

Rievan, Kirst. "Are Foreigners Still Needed in the Age of Indigenous Mission? Roles, Strategies and Reflections for Outsiders in Local Contexts." *Lausanne Global Analysis* 10, no. 4 (July 2021). https://lausanne.org/content/lga/2021-07/are-foreigners-still-needed-in-the-age-of-indigenous-mission.

Further Reading

Elmer, Duane. *Cross-Cultural Conflict*. Downers Grove, IL: InterVarsity Press, 1993.

Grow2Serve. "Intentional Intercultural Teams." Accessed January 14, 2023. https://www.missiontools.org/resources/intentional-multi-cultural-teams/.

Lingenfelter, Sherwood. *Leading Cross-Culturally: Covenant Relationships for Effective Christian Leadership*. Grand Rapids, MI: Baker, 2008.

Moreau, Scott. "Becoming a Healthy Multi-Cultural Team: How to Reach the 'Effective Synergy' Phase." *Lausanne Global Analysis* 8, no. 2 (March 2019). https://lausanne.org/content/lga/2019-03/becoming-a-healthy-multi-cultural-team.

Chapter 20

Majority World Partnerships in Mission

Ken Katayama

They look at each other in the small living room in the same house where just a month ago John, an international missionary, had led a significant Bible training about communion. Then the leaders of fifteen small house churches in a highly persecuted Muslim country in Central Asia celebrated their first Lord's Supper together. Now John and his family were gone. The local government ordered all foreigners to leave the country. Though they were missing John and his family, the house church could not stop. They remembered the words of Jesus: "I will build my church, and the gates of hell shall not prevail against it" (Matt 16:18 ESV). The church leaders prayed as they faced the challenge of losing most of their international help.

A couple of months passed. The exodus of foreigners was complete. Now, these local house-church leaders were responsible to shepherd small communities of believers spread throughout the country. Musa, one of the leaders, remembered a friend in Moldova who had experience leading a small church planting movement there.

Similar to the Macedonian man asking for the Apostle Paul's help (Acts 16:9 ESV), Musa contacted his longtime friend Dima in Moldova and asked him for help. As a former Soviet Union republic, Moldova remained part of the Common International States (CIS) and they not only spoke the common Russian language but also were able to come and go under the government's radar to help those in Musa's country.

Several months later, in the Spring of 2008, Musa's Moldovan friend Dima arrived in Central Asia. Together they formally established a local house-church network consisting of believers meeting in fifteen different houses. They also formalized a partnership focused on the development of new leadership and multiplication of these house churches.

From 2008 to 2021, these partnerships have borne much fruit for the glory of God! After thirteen years of partnership, the Lord has used this relationship to multiply the fifteen house churches into 198 new house churches organized into three different local church networks within this Muslim Central Asian country.

This story demonstrates a successful Majority World partnership in missions. Though I have changed the names for security reasons, the story remains true. This partnership with local church leaders in Central Asia is one out of many partnership stories that Crossover Global has been privileged to see develop over the last two decades.

Though Crossover Global is not the focus of this article, it is important to introduce the organization in order to provide context for the lessons I have learned and seek to present here. Crossover Global, a church planting organization established in 1987 in the USA, seeks to plant multiplying churches among unreached peoples of the world. The founders set a clear direction that ministry is not from the "West to the rest, but from the reached to the unreached." Today, Crossover Global's team has planted over thirty-three hundred churches among 201 unreached peoples in thirty-four countries. Through a coordinated effort together with locals, this has resulted in seventeen different church planting networks.

This chapter seeks to share Crossover Global's principles and practices for partnership based on the lessons learned about strategic partnership with local house-church networks in places such as Azerbaijan, Jordan, India, Nepal, Turkey, and Uzbekistan. These principles and practices are limited in nature since our partnerships are highly focused on church multiplication. My hope is that these principles and practices will give you some applicable ideas and inspire you to seek fruitful kingdom partnerships.

Too Important Not to Try

Partnership is hard. Good and effective partnership is even harder. Most of us in the global family of Christ agree that we are not here to fulfill the Great Commission alone. In fact, a couple of years ago, our association used a tagline that said: "The Great Commission is too big for anyone to accomplish alone and too important not to try to do together."[1]

While partnership is an inspiring concept and the task at hand is urgent, things get complex and challenging at the ground level. Right after my meeting with the leaders of this Central Asian house-church network, many questions arose: How much control should foreigners have over the

---

1 "Great Commission."

partnership? How much money can be given before the relationship gets corrupted? Who gets the credit when the vision is accomplished? Can we trust each other? As we got to know these leaders better, we found they were asking similar questions.

We came to the following conclusions:

Local Church Network	Crossover Global
We desire to be coached, not controlled.	We desire to affirm authority, not take authority.
We desire to give relational authority, not organizational authority.	We desire to extend the kingdom of God with you, not through you.
We desire to be guided, not driven.	We desire to serve you, not to take advantage of you.
	We desire to empower, not enslave.

These affirmations gave us clarity to articulate three main principles that have provided foundational guidance to develop fruitful and long-term partnerships.

Relationship-Based

First, we realized that *partnership should be first and foremost a relationship-based agreement instead of a transaction-based agreement.* In every current partnership, the conversation started based on what we could accomplish together. This foundation is natural, normal, and in some ways the right place to start a conversation, but it is not the right place to start a partnership. We have learned that after an initial exciting exchange of all the possible outcomes we could accomplish together, we need to step back, put our dreams and aspirations on hold and get to know each other.

Relationship building takes time. Establishing a partnership solely based on dreams and ideas could be the beginning of the end. Relationship-based partnerships are more fruitful in the long run. The road ahead for any partnership is bumpy. Relationships are based on trust, and relationships will hold us together. Relationship-based partnerships help us to know our partners' character, priorities, and competencies. These three components play an important role in deciding if a relationship and partnership should move forward.

Vision-Focused

Second, a *partnership should be vision-focused instead of activity-focused*. As non-profits, we have a tendency to overemphasize activities. It makes sense. Activities are where stories take place, lives get changed, and eternity becomes real. Because of this gravitational pull, many partnerships are solely based on activities rather than outcomes. The potential problem ahead is that outcomes, not activities, are the strategic core of a partnership. Together we can accomplish more (outcome) than what we could accomplish alone!

As Westerners, we cannot help but bring our cultural filter and logic to the table. We are tempted to have a mindset that says: "We spent all this money and time to come to visit you, so let's make the deal!" It is highly important to make sure that we create clarity during this process. Again, this takes time, especially when dealing with a cross-cultural partner. It can be the most frustrating part of a partnership agreement. Since clarity is so important, we must not make shortcuts or compromises.

As partners, we must also be patient. We must be students of the local culture. As much as possible, we must learn how our partners think and what they value. For instance, our local partners are from an honor-shame culture, so we had to adapt our vocabulary accordingly.

Nothing is more frustrating than coming back from an overseas trip excited about a newly established partnership just to find out that what you understood is not the same thing that the local partner was saying. Ensuring clarity on terminology, expectations, and outcomes is critical for a smooth and successful partnership.

Values-Driven

Lastly, a *partnership should be values-driven instead of strategic-driven*. As a leader, you probably ask two questions in order to prioritize your time and demands—why and what? On every team, there is a person who thinks about the *how*, and it would be wise to welcome their help when forming cross-cultural partnerships.

Peter Drucker, management consultant and influential thinker, is well known for saying that culture eats strategy for breakfast. Understanding the culture (values) in which a given partnership will be conducted is vital, especially when dealing with a cross-cultural partnership where both parties will need to learn a new culture for communicating effectively, making decisions, and managing financial and material resources.

This is where trust comes into play. A relationship-based partnership will give you and your partner permission to ask *how* questions with freedom. I seldom hear someone saying that they were once well-connected and had great synergy with their cross-cultural partners but woke up one day no longer believing they were called to accomplish the same vision. Most of the time, a broken partnership has to do with differences in ministry philosophy and biblical beliefs that were there from the beginning.

Just like every agency or local church, a partnership will eventually develop its own culture. That culture will grow out of your relationship and interaction with each other. It will be based on your history together, meals shared, meetings, and how you handle successes and failures. A values-driven partnership works through the details and hard questions in areas such as communication, ministry philosophy, and handling of financial resources.

Long-Term Partnership

As you read these principles, you may have realized that Crossover Global's approach to partnership is a long progress. We intentionally choose to operate in this way. Time is the foundational building block through which these relationship-based, vision-focused, and values-driven partnerships are built. The graph below helps to summarize these partnership principles:

LONG TERM PARTNERSHIPS		
Relationship-Based	Vision-Focused	Values-Driven
Who?	What?	How?
TRUST	**CLARITY**	**CULTURE**
Character Competencies Priorities	Terminology Expectations Outcomes	Communication Philosophy / Methods Finances

The Art of Coordination

A dear friend of mine challenged my thinking a few years ago when he boldly said, "Collaboration is overrated! Coordination is underrated!" At first, I did not realize how deeply profound my friend's idea was. I carried his words for a couple of months and asked the leadership team at Crossover Global about the idea. My friend gave us clear terminology for our partnership model—coordination!

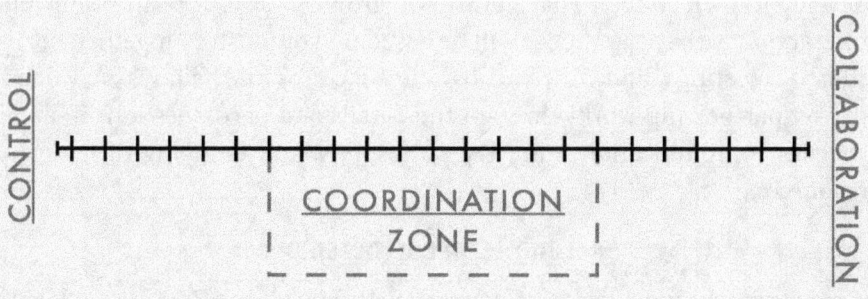

I am Brazilian-born, so I have observed how Europeans in southern Brazil exercised control over ministries. I am afraid that my personal experience in Brazil with European missionaries was not an exception. In missions, it seems that collaboration developed as a reaction against control. As mission strategies moved from a top-down model to a flat model of collaboration, kingdom progress was made, as evidenced by the emergence of think-tanks, networking conferences, and global consultations. But unfortunately, moving from one extreme to the other has also had negative consequences. For instance, a lot of good ideas have been considered and discussed in network meetings, but their implementation has often been lacking. The mentality "no one gets the credit" normally equals "nothing gets done."

At Crossover Global, we have learned that the proper tension between control and collaboration is a better model to use when partnering with those in the Majority World. We call it the Art of Coordination because it swings back and forth. Control and collaboration interact and complement each other.

A good example of how this works is in our human bodies, especially the bodies of athletes. It is amazing to see how baseball players can hit a fast ninety-mile-per-hour ball or to see how a professional golfer can hit a ball with such spin, altitude, and distance. When we know people who are very good in such sports, we normally refer to them not as people with hand-eye collaboration or hand-eye control, but with hand-eye coordination.

Following Webster's definition, we understand coordinating efforts to be "the process of organizing people or groups so that they work together properly and well; the harmonious functioning of parts for effective results."[2] We have learned that for a great partnership to exist, we do not need to make a decision about who will or will not be in charge. We learned that by remaining true to who we are and allowing our partners to be true to who they are, more kingdom work could be accomplished. Just like in Paul's example in 1 Corinthians 12, an eye doesn't become a hand or a hand become an eye in order to work together. The power is in the ability to coordinate with each other's strengths and weaknesses.

These partnerships with local church leaders around the world have resulted in the establishment of thousands of new churches among unreached people groups. None of us could have accomplished this much alone. Due to our relationship-based focus, several of these network leaders have passed the local house-church network on to the next generation and have joined our staff. Of these leaders, two are leading a local office of operations for Crossover Global. They are deploying cross-cultural church planters from the churches we established together over the years to reach other near-culture unreached people groups.

Conclusion

As we reflect on these principles and practices, we are constantly learning. This has been our experience as we try to cut through all the noise around us and intentionally develop fruitful kingdom partnerships. As I close, let me share a list of questions that we ask before beginning a new partnership.

- Do I know them well enough to trust them?
- What do I know about his/her family?
- What other types of partners do they have?
- Would we partner with their partners?
- Could I release full control to their local leadership?
- Would I ever consider recruiting them to be part of my organization?
- Would I have them as staff members in my church?

---

2 Merriam Webster, s.v. "coordination."

- Is what I am saying the same thing as what they are hearing?
- What are the promises we are making each other? Do we have it on paper?
- Are our expectations of each other clearly stated?
- Do we have multiple people from both teams giving their buy-in and agreement?
- What are the outcomes we hope for?
- How long is this partnership?
- How do we evaluate? Measure?
- When and how many times will progress be reported? Who will do the reporting?
- Can we cancel the agreement? When? How?

Bibliography

Merriam Webster s.v. "coordination (n.)," accessed January 13, 2023. https://www.merriam-webster.com/dictionary/coordination.

"The Great Commission: Big and Important!" Missio Nexus, September 20, 2014, https://missionexus.org/the-great-commission-big-important/.

Part Six

Final Reflections

Chapter 21

A Piece in God's Global Mission Puzzle

Steve Richardson

As excited as I am to be part of Columbia International University's 100th anniversary celebration, part of me wonders, *might this be our final big anniversary celebration*? Someday—maybe soon—the Great Commission will be fulfilled, and the Lord Jesus will return. At that point, our opportunity to participate in global missions will be over. Will we have any regrets? We *know* the story of the church ultimately ends in glory with the nations worshipping before the throne of God (Rev 7:9 ESV). Do we *live* accordingly?

I tend to think of my life in chapters. I grew up on the island of New Guinea, with a front-row seat to watch the gospel transform the Sawi people from headhunters and cannibals to evangelists sending out missionaries to other tribes. The story is told in detail in my father's book *Peace Child*. It was an incredible privilege to be part of missions history in that context.

My time at CIU was another important chapter in my life. I wanted to participate in global missions, but I needed a launching pad. As a senior in high school, I asked my father for advice because he had visited a lot of Christian colleges. He recommended CIU as "a great place to prepare for global missions" that had a "special spirit." I found him to be correct. At CIU, I learned leadership skills and how to handle God's word. I practiced ministry in a variety of settings and strengthened my life disciplines. In the process, I met my wife, Arlene. We developed deep friendships with like-minded people and dreamed together about where we might serve God in his Great Commission.

When Arlene and I left CIU, we didn't know what the future held, but we trusted God and prayerfully pursued his big-picture plan for our lives. A fellow CIU student told me, "You take Indonesia, I'll take India." There may have been some hubris wrapped up in that statement, but also a lot of faith. And God has, indeed, done great things since then. Arlene and I led a team that planted churches in one of the biggest unreached people groups in the world.

In each chapter of my life, I see God's clear fingerprints. Redemptive history also has chapters, and corporately, as the church, we have an exciting chapter ahead. Jesus told his disciples, "Whoever believes in me will also do the works that I do; and greater works than these will he do, because I am going to the Father" (John 14:12 ESV). I'm sure the disciples found that prediction hard to understand or imagine, yet today we can see how the spirit of God is truly on the move in the world. We have the privilege of observing and participating in what feels like the most exciting and most fruitful chapter in the history of global missions!

So, what can we expect as we look to the future? It would be presumptuous for me to suggest I have a clear view of what's coming. Our God is a God of surprises. But let me mention some of the bigger dynamics at play in the world today, which I believe will continue to shape global missions in the next chapter of redemptive history.

Multiplication

Though many believers may not realize it, we are currently living in the midst of the greatest spiritual harvest the world has ever known. The church is not only growing, but it's also multiplying. Just fifty years ago, relatively few of the fifteen hundred tribes in the area of New Guinea where I grew up had access to the gospel. Now, almost every one of them has churches. The number of evangelical believers in the world grew by almost 500 percent between 1900 and 2020.[1] In Latin America, evangelicals grew from 825,000 to 51 million in that same span of one hundred twenty years, while the church in Africa grew from 1.8 million to 161 million.[2]

As Kenneth Scott Latourette noted, "No fact of history is more amazing than the spread of the influence of Jesus."[3] This is a season of growth and multiplication for the body of Christ, and I'm confident it will continue in the decades ahead. God is at work! Prepare to be amazed.

Mobilization

The worldwide growth of the church is an exciting development. But that's not all. We're also seeing God's answer to the prayer Jesus instructed us to pray, asking that he would "send out laborers into his harvest" (Luke 10:2 ESV). The church isn't just multiplying around the world, it's also discovering

---

[1] Johnson and Zurlo, *World Christian Encyclopedia*, 25.

[2] Johnson and Zurlo, 25.

[3] Latourette, *Unquenchable Light*, xi.

the joy and privilege of participation in the Great Commission. In 1900, South Korea had sixty-four hundred evangelical Christians.[4] Today, they have sent out thirty thousand missionaries.[5] Just thirty years ago, there were only a handful of Mongolian believers. Today there are at least nine thousand[6] and some of them serve as missionaries with Pioneers. I know of one African mission organization that has sent out seven hundred workers to thirty-six countries. Between 2005 and 2020, 3,158 people groups were engaged for the first time by 5,159 missionary teams.[7]

Missions is no longer from "the West to the rest." Now it's everyone to everywhere. And that's wonderful news, because the Great Commission was given to the entire church, not just a few specialists. As G. Allen Fleece put it, "Regardless of the particular work God has for each of us to do, the one aim of us all in our particular job for the Lord must be the evangelization of the whole world."[8] The key question for believers all around the world is not, *should I be involved in missions?* But, *how can I most strategically align my background, talents, and resources with God's redemptive plan?*

It's challenging for many people to keep the reality of our progress in the Great Commission in appropriate tension with the staggering remaining need. We tend to focus on one at the expense of the other. While the progress of missions over the last century is exciting, much work remains to be done. For example, Chad, in Central Africa, currently has eighty unreached people groups.[9] The Caucuses, between the Black and Caspian Seas, are home to 128 more.[10] Indonesia has 240 unreached people groups.[11] India has more than two thousand unreached groups, representing 1.3 billion people who don't have access to the gospel.[12] Let's be encouraged, but also very sober about the scale of the remaining task. There is much yet to be done.

---

4 Johnson and Zurlo, *World Christian Encyclopedia*, 738.
5 Johnson and Zurlo, 743.
6 Johnson and Zurlo, 540.
7 Finishing the Task, "Global 2020 Update."
8 Fleece, quoted in C. Gordon Olson, *What in the World*, 64.
9 Joshua Project, "Country: Chad."
10 Joshua Project, "People Cluster: Caucasus."
11 Joshua Project, "Country: Indonesia."
12 Joshua Project, "Country: India."

Collaboration

It's not just the business world that is globalizing. So is missions. Mindful of the backdrop of global church growth and the remaining massive need, I'm thankful we're in an era where collaboration is the name of the game. We have the benefit of building on what prior generations have accomplished. At Pioneers, one of our joys is to see an increasingly multinational, multicultural workforce. For example, we now support missionaries from eighty passport countries. In fact, some of our teams have included eight or nine nationalities!

In light of the growing participation of the global church in missions, Westerners sometimes feel that our own missionary-sending efforts are becoming unnecessary, or maybe even detrimental. Don't buy that lie. *All* of God's people have a part to play in the Great Commission until the task is complete and Jesus returns. That hasn't changed. But how we can participate in the next chapter is shifting rapidly. In my book *Is the Commission Still Great?* I mention five roles for which Western believers are particularly suited. We can still make a vital contribution to the unfinished task as encouragers, catalysts, connectors, resourcers, and pioneers.[13]

In coming years, Western missionaries will be vastly outnumbered by gospel workers from the Global South, which will provide many exciting opportunities for partnership and collaboration. The Great Commission has always had a global scope. Now it also has a truly global workforce.

Disruption

If you read the news at all, you've probably felt the sense that God is shaking the nations socially, geopolitically, and economically. Missions isn't just accomplished by us being methodical and doing the day-to-day work of evangelism and discipleship, vital as that element is. God is also at work in huge, nation-changing ways to cultivate responsive hearts for the gospel. He often does that through disruption.

A hundred million people—about one in seventy-eight alive today—have been forcibly displaced from their homes because of war, violence, and human rights abuses.[14] Many of them are now more open to the gospel than they've ever been before. Missionaries working in Greece report that about one in ten Afghans who arrive as refugees come to faith in Jesus.

---

13 Richardson, *Is the Commission*, 178–79.
14 UNHCR, "Global Trends."

The Iranian church is also growing rapidly, despite (or perhaps partly because of) persecution and unrest. I've been told that the largest Persian church in the world meets in Jakarta.

I predict that God will continue to shake and disrupt the nations until his redemptive purposes are accomplished. Are we ready for the harvest he is bringing in unlikely places? Are we positioning ourselves to welcome displaced people and introduce them to the God who loves and died for them?

Opposition

Opposition is not a new development in missions. The gospel has an enemy, and he has always done all he can to thwart the advance of the church. I don't expect that to stop until the Lord puts an end to it at his return. The enemy knows his time is short, so his resistance is fierce. Open Doors estimates that sixteen Christians are martyred every day for their faith.[15]

The church will continue to be purified through suffering, and the testimony of persecuted saints will continue to be a powerful force in global missions. One of my good friends in Indonesia came to faith when a woman showed her the scars on her back from when she was beaten for being a Christian. The believer's obvious joy in the gospel, despite her suffering, broke down my friend's resistance, and she finally embraced Jesus. She insisted on being baptized in front of her Muslim village, and today she is a fearless evangelist among her people.

As we "share abundantly" in both Christ's sufferings and comfort, we learn to "rely not on ourselves but on God who raises the dead" (2 Cor 1:5, 9 ESV). Before 1884, Korea was considered impossible to penetrate with the gospel. More than five hundred missionaries are buried in a graveyard in Seoul. They gave their lives with very little fruit. But today, fully 25 percent of Koreans identify themselves as evangelical, and they have sent out thirty thousand missionaries from their midst.[16] The faithfulness and perseverance of generations of missionaries is now paying rich dividends.

I believe opposition to the Great Commission will continue and even strengthen. I also believe the suffering of the church will be a megaphone for the message of hope that sustains us against all odds. While painful, opposition purifies God's people and advances the gospel.

---

15 Hamm, "16 Christians Murdered."

16 Johnson and Zurlo, *World Christian Encyclopedia*, 738–43.

Celebration

For some people, giving away the ending ruins a story, but I take comfort in the many "spoilers" God has provided. We don't know how long it will be until Christ returns, but we are closer than ever to the finish line!

Jesus spoke of the kingdom as a great marriage banquet, a time of celebration for the invited guests. I imagine it as something like the tribal celebrations I've attended commemorating the arrival of the gospel or the completion of a Scripture translation. Entire villages danced and feasted for days. Jesus promised that "people will come from east and west, and from north and south, and recline at table in the kingdom of God" (Luke 13:29 ESV).

Conclusion

So what about us? If I am right, the future of missions involves a growing global church and missionary workforce joining hands to complete the Great Commission amid severe opposition and disruption. So what does that mean for believers today?

First, are your eyes lifted to the harvest fields (John 4:35 ESV)? What are you trusting God for in your current stage of life? And how are you aligning your life with the mission Christ gave us? Are you willing to walk through any door God opens? There is still much to be done in global missions, and the enemy wants to keep you on the sidelines. We are called to be world-changing players, not just spectators.

I treasure a note my father once wrote me: "Your life is a strategy of God unfolding in history." Do you see your life that way? I picture myself as one piece of God's global, eternal puzzle. God is building something far grander than we could ever imagine, and he delights to work through unlikely people, including you and me. Each of us has a unique and important place in the completion of his masterpiece. Don't let your life be a missing piece in that wonderful picture.

Bibliography

Finishing the Task. "Global 2020 Update." Accessed February 8, 2023. https://finishingthetask.com/wp-content/uploads/FTT-Global-2020-Update.pdf.

Hamm, Ryan. "16 Christians Murdered for Following Jesus—Every Day." Global Christian Relief. January 21, 2022. https://globalchristianrelief.org/christian-persecution/stories/16-christians-murdered-for-following-jesus-every-day/.

Johnson, Todd M., and Gina A. Zurlo. *World Christian Encyclopedia*. 3rd ed. Edinburgh: Edinburgh University Press, 2020.

Joshua Project. "Country: Chad." Accessed January 15, 2023. https://joshuaproject.net/countries/CD.

Joshua Project. "Country: India." Accessed January 15, 2023. https://joshuaproject.net/countries/IN.

Joshua Project. "Country: Indonesia." Accessed January 15, 2023. https://joshuaproject.net/countries/ID.

Joshua Project. "People Cluster: Caucasus." Accessed January 15, 2023. https://joshuaproject.net/clusters/157.

Latourette, Kenneth Scott. *The Unquenchable Light*. New York: Harper & Brothers, 1941.

Olson, C. Gordon. *What in the World Is God Doing? The Essentials of Global Missions: An Introductory Guide*. 5th ed. Cedar Knolls, NJ: Global Gospel, 2003.

Richardson, Steve. *Is the Commission Still Great? 8 Myths about Missions and What They Mean for the Church*. Chicago: Moody Publishers, 2022.

UNHCR. "Global Trends." *The UN Refugee Agency*. Accessed January 15, 2023. https://www.unhcr.org/globaltrends.

Contributors

Rick Amos (MS, University of Texas-Dallas) serves with Eurasia Partners Network, coaching leaders to accelerate church growth in Central Europe, Russia, and Central Asia. Previously, he served for ten years in cross-cultural ministry in Hungary and Russia.

Raphael Anzenberger (DMin, Columbia International University, 2011; PhD, Columbia International University, 2020) is a Billy Graham Lausanne scholar who serves as Executive Director of the French-speaking Canadian Baptist Union. Previously, he served for fifteen years as an evangelist, church planter, and missiologist in France. His books include *(re)Discovering the Ministry of the Evangelist*.

Wendy Atkins (MA, Dallas International University; Certificate in Biblical Studies, Columbia International University, 1990) has served with African Inland Mission in a variety of African contexts since 1986. A specialist in arts and trauma ministry, she is an adjunct instructor at Dallas International University's Center for Excellence in World Arts.

William A. Brown (BA, Columbia International University, 1993) has served as pastor of the Église Réformée de Tunisie since 2002. Prior to that, he served for seven years in cross-cultural ministry in France. William has also completed additional studies at Liberty University and Fuller Theological Seminary.

David Cashin (PhD, Stockholm University) is currently professor of intercultural studies and Muslim-Christian relations at Columbia International University. He served for sixteen years in cross-cultural ministry in Bangladesh and Sweden. He has authored five books, including *Muhammad and the People of the Book* and *The Seven Essential Questions of Life*.

Trevor Castor (PhD, Melbourne School of Theology; MA, Columbia International University, 2010; BA, Columbia International University, 2008) serves as the director of the Zwemer Center for Muslim Studies and adjunct professor of Muslim-Christian relations at Columbia International University. He served with Youth with a Mission for seven years and worked among Muslims in South Asia. He is the author of *Narrative Identity: Transnational Practices of Pashtun Immigrants in the United States*.

SEAN CHRISTENSEN (MDiv, Columbia International University, 1998) serves on the global leadership team for training and spiritual vitality with World Team and is the partnership ministry director for Latin America and the Caribbean with World Team. Previously, he served for thirteen years in Haiti as both field director and a professor of New Testament, and for eight years in pastoral ministry in Wisconsin.

VICTOR H. CUARTAS (DMin, Regent University; PhD, Columbia International University, 2019) is the Elmer V. Thompson Chair of Church Planting and professor of intercultural studies at Columbia International University. He also serves in various capacities with Crossover Global. He spent many years in mission and church planting in Colombia before continuing his ministry in the United States and North Africa. Victor's most recent publication is *Hispanic Muslims in the United States*.

ROBIN P. HARRIS (PhD, University of Georgia; MA, Columbia International University, 2001) serves as associate professor of world arts and chair of the Center for Excellence in World Arts at Dallas International University. Previously, she served for ten years among First Nations groups in Canada and Alaska, then in northern Russia. Her books include *Worship and Mission for the Global Church: An Ethnodoxology Handbook* and *Storytelling in Siberia: The Olonkho Epic in a Changing World*.

BILL JONES (DMin, Columbia International University, 1991) currently serves as the chancellor of Columbia International University. Prior to that, he served as CIU's fifth president (2007–2017) and as a professor of evangelism and church planting. In 1987, he founded the mission organization Crossover Global, where he continues to serve. His books include *Putting Together the Puzzle of the Old Testament*, *Putting Together the Puzzle of the New Testament*, *The Ministry Multiplication Cycle*, and *The Scripture's Grand Story through the Old Testament*.

KEN KATAYAMA (MA, Columbia International University, 2021; BA, Columbia International University, 2011), originally from Brazil, serves as the global president and CEO of Crossover Global, a mission organization committed to planting churches among the least reached. Since joining Crossover Global in 1999, Ken has ministered in over thirty countries. His published works include *Hope, 2020,* and *Turkey: Reviving the Land of the Early Church*.

TIMOTHY KEEP (MA, Wesleyan Graduate School for Asia) has served in intercultural ministry for twenty-six years, thirteen of which were in the Philippines. In 2012, Tim founded Shepherds Global Classroom, a ministry serving underserved pastors and Christian leaders in dozens of countries. With his wife Becky, he has authored three books: *Eyes to See: Glimpses of God in the Dark*, *It's All About Obedience: One Woman's Discovery of a Fruitful Life in a Foreign Land*, and *All Is Well: Finding the Great Heart of God When a Child Walks Away*.

DAE-YOUNG LEE (PhD, Jeonbuk National University, Korea; PhD, Columbia International University, 2019) serves as general surgeon, director of the International Health Care Center, and director of the Palliative Care Center at Presbyterian Medical Center, Jeonju, Korea. Previously, he served for thirteen years in intercultural medical ministry in the Arab world. He is the author of *Shalom: God's Ultimate Purpose for the World: Modern Medical Mission in the Islamic Context*.

DANNY MCCAIN (PhD, Bob Jones University; MA, Columbia International University, 1974) serves as a professor of biblical theology in the department of religion and philosophy and the director of the Centre for Conflict Management and Peace Studies, University of Jos in Nigeria where he has served since 1988. He is also the founder and international ambassador of Global Scholars. He is the author of eighteen books, including *Serving God Away from Home* and *To the Ends of the Earth*.

JILL H. MCELHENY (DNP, University of Colorado) is the dean of nursing programs at Columbia International University. She has spent twenty-eight years in the healthcare field and nursing education. She is also a member of the medical disaster team with Samaritan's Purse International Relief and a medical transporter for Samaritan's Purse Children's Heart Project. She is a contributing author to *Nursing as Ministry*.

BRENT MCHUGH (MA, Columbia International University, 2003) serves as the CEO of Christar International. Previously a store operations manager with Walgreens, he has served cross-culturally in Turkey and Spain.

Jairo de Oliveira (MA, Columbia International University, 2017, 2018; PhD, Columbia International University, 2022), originally from Brazil, has served in seven different nations and presently serves among African and Arab refugees in the Middle East. He is the author of fifteen books, including *Changing Stories: Responding to the Refugee Crisis Based on Biblical Theory and Practice*.

Robert J. Priest (PhD, University California-Berkley; BA, Columbia International University, 1979) previously served as professor of mission and anthropology and as the G. W. Aldeen Professor of International Studies at Trinity Evangelical Divinity School. He is a former president of both the American Society of Missiology and the Evangelical Missiological Society. Currently retired, he focuses on research, writing, and conference presentations. His books include *African Christian Leadership*, *The Missionary Family*, and *Effective Engagement in Short-Term Missions*.

Steve Richardson (BA, Columbia International University; MA, Columbia International University, 1985) has been president of Pioneers-USA since 1999. Prior to that, he served in church planting and leadership in Southeast Asia for thirteen years. He is the author of *Is the Commission Still Great?*

Dietrich Schindler (DMin, Fuller Theological Seminary; BA, Columbia International University, 1981) is a TEAM missionary church planter who has started churches in Germany and presently serves as a church planting consultant in Europe. He is the author of *The Jesus Model: Planting Churches the Jesus Way* and *SHIFT: The Road to Level 5 Church Multiplication*.

Bekele Shanko (Doctorate in Global Transformational Leadership, Bakke Graduate University), born and raised in Ethiopia, has served on staff with Cru since 1993 in Ethiopia, southern and eastern Africa, and presently as the vice president for global church movements. He is the author of *Never Alone: From Ethiopian Villager to Global Leader*.

Edward L. Smither (PhD, University of Wales; PhD, University of Pretoria) serves as professor of intercultural studies and history of global Christianity and dean of the College of Intercultural Studies at Columbia International University. Previously, he served for fourteen years in intercultural ministry in North Africa, France, and the United States. His recent books include *Christian Mission: A Concise Global History* and *Mission in the Way of Daniel*.

Jessica A. Udall (PhD, Columbia International University, 2022) serves as professor of intercultural studies at Evangelical Theological College in Addis Ababa, Ethiopia, and adjunct professor of intercultural studies at Columbia International University. She has served in cross-cultural ministry in Ethiopia and among refugees in the United States. She is the author of *Loving the Stranger: Welcoming Immigrants in the Name of Jesus*.

Ted B. Wingo (DMin, Trinity Evangelical Divinity School; BS, Columbia International University, 1978) served in Bible translation among the Tarahumara people of Mexico for twenty-five years with Ethnos 360 (formerly New Tribes Mission). Presently, he serves in mobilization with Ethnos 360 and as an adjunct professor of intercultural studies at Columbia International University.

Zhiqiu Xu (PhD, Boston University) is a professor of theology and administrative dean of the Kepha Institute at Columbia International University. He previously served as a pastor for thirteen years in Massachusetts and has served in short-term missions in China, Hong Kong, Thailand, and England. He is the author of *Natural Theology Reconfigured: Confucian Axiology and American Pragmatism*.

Additional Resources from the Publisher
Visit Us at missionbooks.org

Against the Tide: Mission Amidst the Global Currents of Secularization
  By W. Jay Moon & Craig Ott, editors

Beyond Our Walls: Finding Jesus in the Slums of Jakarta
  By Anita Rahma

Beyond Poverty: Multiplying Sustainable Community Development
  By Terry Dalrymple

Calling on the Prophets: In Christian Witness to Muslims
  By Colin Bearup

Creating Local Arts Together:
  A Manual to Help Communities Reach Their Kingdom Goals
  By Brian Schrag and James R. Krabill, editors

Community Arts for God's Purposes: How to Create Local Artistry Together
  By Brian Schrag

Effective Spiritual Warfare: Wrestling in God's Strength
  By Mary Lou Codman-Wilson

Engaging Islamic Traditions: Using the Hadith in Christian Ministry to Muslims
  By Bernie Power

Journey with Me: Spiritual Formation for Global Workers
  By Herbert F. Lamp, Jr.

Margins of Islam: Ministry in Diverse Muslim Contexts
  By Gene Daniels and Warrick Farah, editors

Missionary Motivations: Challenges from the Early Church
  By Matthew Burden

Multiplying Leaders in Intercultural Contexts: Recognizing and Developing Grassroots Potential
  By Evelyn and Richard Hibbert

New Funding Models for Global Mission: Learning from the Majority World
  By Tim Welch

Practicing Hope: Missions and Global Crises
  By Jerry M. Ireland and Michelle L. K. Raven, editors

Sacred Siblings: Valuing One Another for the Great Commission
  By Sue Eenigenburg and Suzy Grumelot

Stick Figures Save the World
  By Pam Arlund

The Multilingual God: Stories of Translation
  By Steve Fortosis

Village Medical Manual: A Guide to Health Care in Developing Countries
  (*2-volume set*)
  By Mary Vanderkooi

Zúme Training: Multipying Disciples
  By The Zúme Project

Visit Us at missionbooks.org

Reading Hebrews Missiologically
The Missionary Motive, Message, and Methods of Hebrews

Abeneazer G. Urga, Edward L. Smither, and Linda P. Saunders, Editors

The discussion on the theology of mission in the New Testament usually focuses on Jesus and Paul, with minimal attention given to the General Epistles. However, *Reading Hebrews Missiologically* tries to fill that gap and focuses on the theology of mission in the book of Hebrews. The twelve contributors explore the missionary motive, the missionary message, and the missionary method of the Epistle to the Hebrews. | Paperback & ePub

Mission in the Way of Daniel
Empowering Believers to Live into God's Plan

Edward L. Smither

Mission in the Way of Daniel probes mission theology and practice in the Old Testament, exploring the well-known story of Daniel through the lenses of mission history and mission practice. Providing relevant application for contemporary issues like diaspora, power encounters, and divine favor in mission, the themes in *Mission in the Way of Daniel* advance the ongoing conversation about how to do mission. | Paperback & ePub

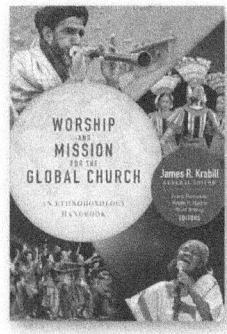

Worship and Mission for the Global Church
An Ethnodoxology Handbook

James R. Krabill, Frank Fortunato, Robin P. Harris, Brian Schrag, Editors

Worship and Mission for the Global Church offers theological reflection, case studies, practical tools, and audiovisual resources to help the global church appreciate and generate culturally appropriate arts in worship and witness. Drawing on the expertise and experience of over one hundred writers from twenty countries, the volume integrates insights from the fields of ethnomusicology, biblical research, worship studies, missiology, and the arts. | Paperback & ePub

www.ingramcontent.com/pod-product-compliance
Lightning Source LLC
Chambersburg PA
CBHW071236070526
44583CB00017B/2213